ISBN EAN-13:   978-1-938117-43-5   [Soft cover Print Edition]

Golden Words Upon Golden Words...For Every Muslim.

"Imaam al-Barbahaaree, may Allaah have mercy upon him said:

May Allaah have mercy upon you! Examine carefully the speech of everyone you hear from in your time particularly. So do not act in haste and do not enter into anything from it until you ask and see: Did any of the Companions of the Prophet, may Allaah's praise and salutations be upon him, speak about it, or did any of the scholars? So if you find a narration from them about it, cling to it, do not go beyond it for anything and do not give precedence to anything over it and thus fall into the Fire.

Explanation by Sheikh Saaleh al-Fauzaan, may Allaah preserve him:

'Do not be hasty in accepting as correct what you may hear from the people especially in these later times. As now there are many who speak about so many various matters, issuing rulings and ascribing to themselves both knowledge and the right to speak. This is especially the case after the emergence and spread of new modern day media technologies. Such that everyone now can speak and bring forth that which is in truth worthless; by this meaning words of no true value - speaking about whatever they wish in the name of knowledge and in the name of the religion of Islaam. It has even reached the point that you find the people of misguidance and the members of the various groups of misguidance and deviance from the religion speaking as well. Such individuals have now become those who speak in the name of the religion of Islaam through means such as the various satellite television channels. Therefore be very cautious!

It is upon you oh Muslim, and upon you oh student of knowledge individually, to verify matters and not rush to embrace everything and anything you may hear. It is upon you to verify the truth of what you hear, asking, 'Who else also makes this same statement or claim?', 'Where did this thought or concept originate or come from?', 'Who is its reference or source authority?'. Asking what are the evidences which support it from within the Book and the Sunnah? And inquiring where has the individual who is putting this forth studied and taken his knowledge from? From who has he studied the knowledge of Islaam?

Each of these matters requires verification through inquiry and investigation, especially in the present age and time. As it is not every speaker who should rightly be considered a source of knowledge, even if he is well spoken and eloquent, and can manipulate words captivating his listeners. Do not be taken in and accept him until you are aware of the degree and scope of what he possesses of knowledge and understanding. As perhaps someone's words may be few, but possess true understanding, and perhaps another will have a great deal of speech yet he is actually ignorant to such a degree that he doesn't actually posses anything of true understanding. Rather he only has the ability to enchant with his speech so that the people are deceived. Yet he puts forth the perception that he is a scholar, that he is someone of true understanding and comprehension, that he is a capable thinker, and so forth. Through such means and ways he is able to deceive and beguile the people, taking them away from the way of truth.

Therefore what is to be given true consideration is not the amount of the speech put forth or that one can extensively discuss a subject. Rather the criterion that is to be given consideration is what that speech contains within it of sound authentic knowledge, what it contains of the established and transmitted principles of Islaam. As perhaps a short or brief statement which is connected to or has a foundation in the established principles can be of greater benefit than a great deal of speech which simply rambles on, and through hearing you don't actually receive very much benefit from.

This is the reality which is present in our time; one sees a tremendous amount of speech which only possesses within it a small amount of actual knowledge. We see the presence of many speakers yet few people of true understanding and comprehension.' "

[The eminent major scholar Sheikh Saaleh al-Fauzaan, may Allaah preserve him- 'A Valued Gift for the Reader Of Comments Upon the Book Sharh as-Sunnah', page 102-103]

My Hijaab, My Path
Pocket Edition
2.

The War on Hijaab

Translated & Compiled By
Umm Mujaahid Khadijah Bint Lacina
al-Amreekiyyah

Table of Contents

A Comprehensive Knowledge Based Compilation on Muslim Women's Role & Dress

*Collected and Translated by
Umm Mujaahid Khadijah Bint Lacina
al-Amreekiyyah*

[Available: **Now**¦ pages: **190+** ¦
price: (Soft cover) **$17.50** ¦
(Hard cover) **$25** ¦
eBook **$9.99**

About the Compiler & Translator

The compiler of this work, Umm Mujaahid Khadijah Bint-Lacina, was raised in a small town in the heartland of middle America. She graduated with honors from the University of Wisconsin only a short time after embracing Islaam and starting to live her life as a committed Muslim. She has been blessed with eight Muslim children she is committed to raising, and is regularly involved in various endeavors to benefit herself, fulfill the responsibility to her household, as well as her community and this blessed Ummah. Additionally, she has, in the years before traveling overseas to seek knowledge of this religion, previously run two successful small business enterprises from home - despite her main occupation as a Muslim mother and wife.

By Allaah's mercy she has been studying Islaam and the Arabic language generally since the time she embraced Islaam almost twenty years ago, and both of these subjects intensively for the past nine years from scholars and students of knowledge in the various centers of learning in Yemen and through the books and recorded lectures of the scholars of the Sunnah from throughout the world. Related to her studies in Arabic, she successfully completed two independent study seminars from the Islamic University of Medina while in the United States before having been blessed with the opportunity to study in Yemen. After beginning her language studies in Yemen with the well-known University of Medina Arabic language series through a private tutor, she then built upon this with the study of related classical works of Arabic Grammar when she started studying at Dar Al-Hadeeth in Mab'ar as well as other recommended works with a focus on works related to the fundamental beliefs of Islaam.

She later was blessed to continue her studies of this deen for three years in Dar Al-Hadeeth in Damaaj where she benefited from several excellent teachers. Among them was her daily class with Umm Salamah, may Allaah preserve her, previously the wife of Sheikh Muqbil, with whom in daily study she completed the work Bulugh al-Maram with the exception of two individual chapters due to illness. There she also benefited from the weekly class of the daughter of Sheikh Muqbil, Umm 'Abdullah, and from the lectures of well-known scholars of Ahlis Sunnah throughout Yemen who would come to address the students at the center. She has always striven to benefit from the people of knowledge in every city where her family resided in Yemen, while always making her home the center of her efforts to both study and teach this perfect religion.

May Allaah forgive us, her, and all the Muslims their errors and shortcomings, and guide us to every matter of belief, statement, and action that pleases Him alone.

Publisher's Introduction

All praise is due to Allaah, Lord of the Worlds, peace and salutations be upon the Messenger of Allaah, his household, his Companions, and all those who follow his guidance until the day of Judgment. To proceed:

In today's world few people would deny that the struggle between western ideals and concepts and the religion of Islaam is expanding and intensifying. The so-called 'war against terrorism' is by design a very pliant and indefinable undertaking, which is said to confront any entity, potential or actual, that threatens modern western societies. Yet the claim often put forward, that they fight not against Islaam, but only against 'extremism'-rings incredibly hollow, as many people increasingly realize that the form of Islaam that they deem as 'acceptable' to them, and 'suitable to modern times', on one hand, and the understanding of Islaam encompassed within the beliefs and commands explicitly found in the Qur'aan, on the other, are two incompatible and contradictory visions. Indeed the Qur'aan, which is acknowledged by all Muslims to be one of the enduring, unalterable sources of Islaam, clearly and explicitly informs us of the true primary motivation, as well as the mechanisms and objectives of those who disbelieve in Islaam in their continuing efforts at both the personal and societal level to combat against and suppress that "Qur'anic" version of the religion of Islaam, Indeed, the Lord of the Worlds states very clearly,

❖ *And they will never cease fighting you until they turn you back from your religion -if they can. And whosoever of you turns back from his religion and dies as a disbeliever, then his deeds will be lost in this life and in the Hereafter, and they will be the dwellers of the Fire. They will abide therein forever.* ❖-(Surah al-Baqarah: 217). The noble scholar Imaam as-Sa'dee, may Allaah have mercy upon him, explained part of this verse saying,

*"The Most High informs us that the disbelievers will never cease fighting against the believers. And their goal is not taking their wealth or killing them; indeed their primary goal is to force them to abandon and turn away from their religion, in order that they eventually become disbelievers after having already practiced the faith of Islaam, which would lead them to also become people of the Hellfire like those disbelievers. They exert all their efforts and capacity towards achieving that objective. Yet we are informed of what, in actuality, they are and are not capable of, as Allaah states, ⟨ **But Allaah will bring His Light to perfection even though the disbelievers hate this.** ⟩-(Surah As-Saff: 8)*

And this is a general description of every disbeliever. They do not cease opposing and fighting others, until they have actually succeeded in making them abandon and turn away from the religion they once stood upon. And it applies especially to the people of the previous revealed scriptures, from the Jews and Christians. Those who spend significantly upon their worldwide organizations and foundations, sending forth callers to propagate their beliefs, sending forth doctors to work in different lands, building schools- all in an effort to attract and win over the peoples of various nations to their religion, and introduce and plant their foreign religion among these different peoples in their lands. They utilize every matter, and put forth every effort within their capacity, to plant and give rise to doubts among those targeted people which would cause them to have misgivings and uncertainties about the truth of their religion...."

This is indeed the reality in which the person of insight sees us standing in the midst of today. Furthermore there is no issue of engagement related to these numerous battles in the present day ideological warfare against Islaam which carries as much open intensity and passion on both sides as the Muslim woman's hijaab and its predominant place as a symbol of the adherence to or abandonment of Islaam as a way of life.

It has been five years since the democratic government of France banned the individual practice of any Muslim woman resident of that land, from wearing personal clothing that included any recognizable form of hijaab in schools and other indicated areas of public life. Yet many Muslims were genuinely surprised in the face of this explicit assault against their "personal rights" as individual citizens and residents in a western democratic country to practice their religion without infringing upon others in any way or form. These Muslims failed to realize what conforms with what Allaah has stated clearly, that the people who would support such measures simply oppose our very way of life, oppose any concrete expression of a distinct and all-encompassing religious identity, and actually desire that we slowly turn away from any comprehensive form of Islaam which may, even potentially, lead to it being increasingly reflected inwardly and outwardly in the individual and collective lives of Muslim women the world over. This is unfortunately true despite the ever echoing assertions of a commitment to "freedom", "liberty", "self determination", and the "right to individual self expression" which western nations claim to be the guardians of and which they allegedly hope to "enlighten" the Muslim World with. With this ban on hijaab, and the failure of other western countries to vigorously condemn it, many were in fact saying, "*We believe in freedom...but not that kind of freedom*", "*We support the right of self-determination and personal liberty...well...except in regard to Islaam.*"

This documented and evident reality, the war against hijaab, is seen in today's world at various levels, because of that which it invariably represents. It is one of the many fronts which have been opened directly, and more often indirectly, to struggle against any tangible and consistent expression of independent identity by today's Muslims. Their efforts to eradicate and, more significantly, to corrupt and alter hijaab is felt at multiple levels of society, openly and subtly, firstly in their own lands and then additionally as required by their overall objectives, in Muslim countries. Furthermore, their focus upon gradually changing hijaab, and their success in facilitating the adoption of a compromise version of "fashion hijaab", is likewise part of their general attempt to fashion a new "alternate" form of "acceptable" Islaam. Yet in addition to the previously mentioned verse, Allaah has also said to us, ❧*So obey not the deniers. They wish that you should compromise with them, so they too would compromise with you* ☙-(Surah Qalam: 8-9)

This compilation effectively addresses these defining issues on several levels, including the essential core issue of what is the basis upon which the role and purpose of the Muslim woman is defined- yesterday, today, and tomorrow. Is it the guidance found within the Qur'aan, the eternal, uncreated word of the Creator and Sustainer of the universe and the preserved clarifying example of His Final Messenger (may Allaah's praise and salutations be upon him)? Or is it the newly emergent yet ever changing body of western values based upon a rejection of the true nature of the Qur'aan as revelation? In this work, '*My Hijaab, My Path*' the compiler has done an excellent job of incorporating material that addresses these numerous issues and questions, explains the true guidelines regarding hijaab, and has brought clarity and insight to the principles involved; not merely from opinion, experience, or personal views, but by referring to the works of those people who are the only inheritors and successors of the Last Messenger of Islaam upon earth, the scholars. The scholars referred to are from those known for their depth of knowledge of the sources of Islaam. This book is intended for the Muslim woman who truly wishes to hold fast to the guidance of Islaam, not surrendering it for anyone or anything. Her adherence to Islaam despite the storm of misguidance focused against her, upon sincerity and knowledge, is sufficient for her true success as a believer in Islaam. Due to this, the esteemed scholar Imaam as-Sa'dee concludes his explanation of the first mentioned verse by saying,

"*However, a promise has been given by Allaah the Most High, who is the One who Himself blessed the believers with the religion of Islaam, has chosen for those who believe in Him-this priceless religion, and perfected this religion for them. Indeed, He completed His favor upon them by establishing for them the most valuable of things- their religion. Similarly He abandons and turns away from everyone who desires to extinguish the light of His true religion, and causes their intrigues to become caught in their very throats- while bringing victory to His religion and elevating His word. And certainly these verses correctly reflect the true state of the disbelievers, meaning those who are present today from them, ❦ Verily, those who disbelieve spend their wealth to hinder people from the Path of Allaah, and so will they continue to spend it. But in the end it will become an anguish for them, and then they will be overcome. While those who disbelieve will gathered in Hell. ❦*-(Surah Al-Anfal: 36)"

As such, victory in confronting the war against hijaab has already been won by every believing woman who acknowledges the true sources of Islaam, and then learns and practices, upon evidence, each aspect of the guidance of Islaam as found in the Book of Allaah, and the authentic Sunnah of her Prophet ﷺ. Victory has already been given to her by Allaah The Exalted, in her efforts to adhere to the noble examples of the first believers, men and women, and firmly and steadily follow in their footsteps. We hope that the publication of this book acts as a small support and assistance in that for every sincere Muslim woman who truly wants that victory. And the success is from Allaah.

Abu Sukhailah Khalil Ibn-Abelahyi
Taalib al-Ilm Educational Resources

Compilers Introduction (Pocket Edition)

All praise is due to Allaah Alone. We praise Him, seek His help, and ask His forgiveness. We seek refuge in Allaah from the evil of our souls, and the adverse consequences of our deeds. Whomsoever Allaah guides, there is none who can misguide him, and whoever He misguides, there is none who can guide him.

I bear witness that there is nothing worthy of worship except for Allaah; He is alone and has no partners. I bear witness and testify that Muhammad, may Allaah's praise and salutations be upon him and his family, is His perfect worshipper, and messenger.

Oh you who believe! Fear Allaah, as He deserves, and die not except as Muslims. -(Surat al-'Imraan, Ayat 102)
Oh mankind! Fear your Lord, Who created you from a single soul, and from him, He created his wife, and from these two, He created multitudes of men and women. Fear Allaah, from Whom you demand your mutual rights, and do not cut off the ties of kinship. Verily, Allaah is Ever-Watcher over you. -(Surat an-Nisaa', Ayat 1)
Oh you who believe! Fear Allaah, and say righteous speech. He will direct you to do righteous deeds, and He will forgive you your sins. And whoever obeys Allaah and His Messenger has indeed achieved the ultimate success. -(Surat al-Ahzaab, Ayat 70-71)

As to what follows: then the best of speech is the speech of Allaah, and the best guidance is the guidance of Muhammad, may Allaah's praise and salutations be upon him and his family. And the worst of affairs are newly invented matters (in the religion), and every newly invented matter is a misguidance, and every misguidance is in the Hellfire.

To Proceed:

Alhamdulillah, let us look again at the words of the Prophet, may Allaah's praise and salutations be upon him and his family, above:

"The best of speech is the speech of Allaah, and the best guidance is the guidance of Muhammad", may Allaah's praise and salutations be upon him and his family.

These are the sources from which we must take our religion. The Book of Allaah, and the Sunnah of His final Messenger, Muhammad ibn 'Abdullah, may Allaah's praise and salutations be upon him and his family- and we base our understanding of these things on the understanding of the righteous predecessors of the first three generations, alhamdulillah, rather than on our own understandings. The people who may claim this are many, and yet many of them are not actually calling to the true religion of Islaam. Rather, they are calling to Islaam based on their ideas and desires, an Islaam which they twist and mold into the form that best suits their goals, and the goals of the enemies of Islaam, and ultimately, the goals of the accursed *Shaytaan*.

How then, do we know who is calling to the true Islaam?

It is important to understand that, though there is a lot of confusion in the Muslim world, and has been throughout its history, there has always been a group of people that has continued upon the Straight Path of Islaam, as revealed by Allaah to his last Prophet and Messenger, Muhammad ibn 'Abdullaah, praise and salutations be upon him. Distinguished scholars such as Imaam al-Bukhaaree, Imaam Muslim, Imaam Ahmad Ibn Hanbal, Imaam ash-Shaafi'ee, Imaam Maalik, Imaam ash-Shawkaani, Ibn Katheer, and others have carried the banner of Islaam through the ages so that today we can still follow our religion as it was revealed, in all of its perfection, alhamdulillah.

Allaah, the Most High, says in His Noble Book, ❖ *This day I have perfected your religion for you, completed My Favor upon you, and have chosen for you Islaam as your religion* ❖-(Surat al-Maaidah, from Ayat 3)

Allaah gave us our religion in its complete and perfect form- it is not for us to change or recreate it to fit our own ideas and desires, or to conform to the "norm" of the societies around us.

Allaah perfected Islaam for us, and He has always sent people throughout the ages to make sure that the religion is preserved in the form in which it was revealed and originally practiced. This group has many names, including *Ahl-as-Sunnah wa al-Jamaa'ah*, and *as-Salafiyyeen*, but the important thing is that they adhere to the Qur'aan as well as the Sunnah of Prophet Muhammad, praise and salutations be upon him, according to the understanding of the first three generations of Islaam. These were the people who were nurtured at the hand of Allaah's Messenger, praise and salutations be upon him, and his Companions, and so on down through the generations. And, as we must understand the *deen* of al-Islaam with the proofs, I will mention some of them here.

First, from the book of Allaah; *al-Haafidh* ibn Katheer mentions in his *tafseer* of the Qur'aan the explanation of the verse regarding the one who leaves the way of the first believers, which is found in Surat an-Nisaa':

❖ *And whoever contradicts and opposes the Messenger after the right path has been shown clearly to him, and follows other than the believers' way, We shall keep him in the path he has chosen, and burn him in Hell. What an evil destination!* ❖ –(Surat an-Nisaa', Ayat 115)

❧ *And whoever contradicts and opposes the Messenger after the right path has been shown clearly to him.* ❧ This refers to whoever intentionally takes a path other than the path of the Law revealed to the Messenger, after the truth has been made clear, apparent and plain to him.

Allaah's statement, ❧*...and follows other than the believers' way...* ❧ *refers to a type of conduct that is closely related to contradicting the Messenger. This contradiction could be in the form of contradicting a text (from the Qur'aan or Sunnah) or contradicting what the ummah (nation) of Muhammad has agreed on. The ummah of Muhammad is immune from error when they all agree on something, a miracle that serves to increase their honor, due to the greatness of their Prophet. There are many authentic ahaadeeth on this subject.*

Allaah warned against the evil of contradicting the Prophet and his ummah, when He said, ❧ *We shall keep him in the path he has chosen, and burn him in Hell- what an evil destination!* ❧ *meaning, when one goes on this wicked path, We will punish him by making the evil path appear good in his heart, and will beautify it for him so that he is tempted further."*

The Messenger of Allaah, praise and salutations be upon him and his family, made clear the importance of adhering to his guidance and that of the rightly guided predecessors in the following authentic hadeeth, on the authority of al-Irbaad ibn Saaryah who said, *{Allaah's Messenger, may Allaah's praise and salutations be upon him, gave us an admonition which caused our eyes to shed tears and the hearts to fear, so we said, "O Messenger of Allaah, may Allaah's praise and salutations be upon him, this is as if it were a farewell sermon, so with what do you counsel us?"*
So he, may Allaah's praise and His salutations be upon him, said, I have left you upon clear guidance, its night is like its day, no one deviates from it except one who is destroyed, and whoever lives for some time

from amongst you will see great differing. So stick to what you know from my Sunnah and the Sunnah of the rightly guided caliphs. Cling to that with your molar teeth, and stick to obedience even if it is to an Abyssinian slave since the believer is like the submissive camel; wherever he is led, he follows.}

(An authentic hadeeth found in *"Sunan Abu Daawood"* 4607, *"Sunan Ibn Majah"* 43 and 44, *"Sunan at-Tirmidhi"* 2676, *"al-Musnad Ahmad"* vol. 4/126 and other collections. The wording is that of at-Tirmidhi)

And in another authentic hadeeth:

{My ummah will split into seventy three sects, all of them in the Fire except one and it is al-Jamaa'ah.} It was said, "Who are they, O Messenger of Allaah?" He, praise and salutations be upon him, replied, {That which I and my Companions are upon today.}

(Authentic hadeeth reported by at-Tirmidhi (no.2643), al-Laalikaa'ee in *"as-Sunnah"* (no.147) and others)

We can see how the Companions, may Allaah be pleased with all of them, realized this in their lives, by looking at the following *athaar* from their time, may Allaah be pleased with all of them.

'Amr ibn Salmah said: We used to sit by the door of 'Abdullah ibn Mas'ood before the morning prayer, so that when he came out we would walk with him to the masjid. One day Abu Moosaa al-Ash'aree came to us and said, "Has Abu 'Abdur-Rahman come out yet?" We replied, "No." So he sat down with us until he came out. When he came out, we all stood along with him, so Abu Moosaa said to him, "O Abu 'Abdur-Rahman! I have just seen something in the mosque which I deemed to be evil, but all praise is for Allaah, I did not see anything except good." He inquired, "Then

*what is it?" (Abu Moosaa) replied, "If you live you will see it. I
saw in the masjid people sitting in circles awaiting the prayer. In
each circle they had pebbles in their hands and a man would say
'Repeat Allaahu Akbar a hundred times.' So they would repeat
it a hundred times. Then he would say, 'Say laa ilaaha illallaah
a hundred times.' So they would say it a hundred times. Then he
would say, 'Say subhaanallaah a hundred times.' So they would
say it a hundred times." (Ibn Mas'ood) asked, "What did you say
to them?" (Abu Moosaa) said, "I did not say anything to them.
Instead I waited to hear your view or what you declared." (Ibn
Mas'ood) replied, "Would that you had ordered them to count
up the evil deeds they acquired and assured them that their good
deeds would not be lost!"*

*Then we went along with him (Ibn Mas'ood) until he came to
one of these circles and stood and said, "What is this which I
see you doing?" They replied, "O Abu 'Abdur-Rahman! These
are pebbles upon which we are counting takbeer, tahleel and
tasbeeh." He said, "Count up your evil deeds. I assure you that
none of your good deeds will be lost. Woe to you, O ummah of
Muhammad, praise and salutations be upon him! How quickly
you go to destruction! These are the Companions of your Prophet
and they are widespread. There are his clothes which have not
yet decayed and his bowl which is unbroken. By Him in Whose
Hand is my soul! Either you are upon a religion better guided
than the Religion of Muhammad, praise and salutations be
upon him, or you are opening the door of misguidance." They
said, "O Abu 'Abdur-Rahman! By Allaah, we only intended
good." He said, "How many there are who intend good but do
not achieve it. Indeed Allaah's Messenger said to us, "A people
will recite the Qur'aan but it will not pass beyond their throats."
By Allaah! I do not know, perhaps most of them are from you."
Then he left them.*

*Umar ibn Salmah (the sub-narrator) said: We saw most of those
people fighting against us on the day of Nahrawaan, along with
the Khawaarij.*

(Ad-Daarimi in his *"Sunan"* (1/79) Authenticated by Sheikh Saleem al-Hilaalee)

One of the loudest calls today, from the disbelievers as well many misguided individuals within Islaam, is that call to change the *hijaab*, or the Muslim women's dress, or to discard it all together. People with no firm grounding in religious knowledge write books and articles concerning women in the Qur'aan, or the rights of the Muslim women, and they base that which they present upon their own intellect, ideas, and desires, as well as upon that which was said by ignorant, misguided, or evil people other than them, who have been falsely held up as scholars amongst the people. The vast majority of these writers and callers make a point of addressing the issue of the *hijaab* directly. Often they claim it is not from Islaam, or that the form it takes today in many Muslim countries such as Saudi Arabia and Yemen is extreme and unnecessary. This is despite the clear evidences to the contrary, evidences that anyone with a sound intellect can read and understand.

I ask that Allaah correct my mistakes, preserve my intention, and accept this work from me, and I pray that the Muslim *ummah* in general, and my Muslim sisters specifically, benefit from it.

Sheikh Muhammad al-Imaam says, *"Books are authored, and conferences are established which in truth are part of the plots, and they recruit for this purpose some of the male and female teachers, the administrators and other than them from those with diseased hearts. They seize the person who is ignorant of their deception from the callers, the preachers, the scholars, the individuals, and other than them. These individuals then say concerning the hijaab and those that wear it various things which indicate their tremendous wickedness, and the magnitude of their deception. From that which they say concerning the hijaab itself:*

"Shackles", "a tent", "shroud of the dead", "a foolish custom", "a Bedouin practice", and other than that. And from their speech concerning those who wear the hijaab: "Feeble minded women", "demons", "dark tombs", "inferior or old fashioned women", "one who is deformed", "fairy tale women", "diseased women", "crows", and other than that.

There is a multitude of these distortions and slanderous sayings. Callers to depravity bring these numerous doubts to the Muslims, with the intention of influencing people through them, and causing them to fall into their traps. They then make them the means for them to spread this, their call..." (End of quote from Sheikh Muhammad al-Imaam)

I ask that Allaah correct my mistakes, preserve my intention, and accept this work from me, and I pray that the Muslim *ummah* in general, and my Muslim sisters specifically, benefit from it. Any good in this work is from Allaah, alone, who has no partners, and any evil is from myself and the accursed *Shaytaan*.

Umm Mujaahid Khadijah Bint Lacina al-Amreekiyyah as-Salafiyyah

The War Against al-Hijaab

Introduction of
Sheikh Muhammad al-Imaam,
may Allaah preserve him

All Praise is due to Allaah, and I bear witness that there is no God worthy of worship except Allaah, and I bear witness that Muhammad is his Slave and Messenger, praise and salutations be upon him, and on his family, and his companions.

As for what follows:

This is a summarized treatise, encompassing both the exposure and clarification of the war which has been established by the secular communists, the secular liberals, as well as their partners from the callers who make Islaam a riding animal for themselves in order to achieve their filthy objective against the Islamic *hijaab* in the Muslim lands. They proceed in the warfare against the *hijaab* along the path which the enemies of Islaam from the Jews and the Christians have mapped out for them. They make preparations for that, and they put to use every means which is at their disposal for the war against the *hijaab*, in newspapers, magazines, cinema, theatre and stories, and novels. Books are authored, and conferences are established which in truth are part of the schemes, and they recruit for this purpose some of the male and female teachers, the administrators and other than them from those with diseased hearts. They seize the person who is ignorant of their deception from the callers, the preachers, the scholars, the individuals, and other than them. They say concerning the *hijaab* and those who wear it various things which indicate the tremendous extent of their wickedness, and the magnitude of their deception.

From that which they say concerning the *hijaab* itself: "Shackles", "a tent", "shroud of the dead", "a foolish custom", "a Bedouin practice", and other than that.

27

And from their speech concerning those who wear the *hijaab:* "Feeble minded women", "demons", "dark tombs", "inferior or old fashioned women", "one who is deformed", "fairy tale women", "ill women", "crows", and other than that.

There is a multitude of these distortions and slanderous sayings. Callers to depravity bring these numerous doubts to the Muslims, with the intention of influencing people through them, and causing them to fall into their traps. They then make them the means for them to spread this, their call. They have taken more than half a century in their spreading of this. Then, when they saw that they were not successful with this plot, they came to further utilize violent and harsh means, including degrading the women's *hijaab* and removing it by force, and passing laws concerning that. They think that by this process they will reach their goals, and achieve through it that which they dream of in their hearts concerning the eradication of the *hijaab* in all of its shapes and forms. They are surprised by the steadfastness of the Muslim woman, and the return of many of them who had not been strict concerning wearing the *hijaab* (to wearing it). And when they saw that this was the case, then they undertook a third additional path. This third path is to change the form of the *hijaab* itself, in order to dilute and diminish the legislated *hi*jaab, and to display it with an attractive appearance.

Thus, as these enemies have proceeded upon these paths of doing away with this weighty legislated matter of the *hijaab*, I saw that it was appropriate to describe these three types of warfare in order to make clear the significance of its deception to the Muslims in general, and the women in particular. As such the following is a clarification of these three types of campaigns.

I have named the treatise, "*The War against al-Hijaab: The First, The Second, The Third*". By Allaah, I ask that He grants success to Islaam and the Muslims by means of this treatise, and to place acceptance of it on the earth. Verily He is the Guardian of that and the One who has Power over it.

Written by Abu Nasr Muhammad ibn 'Abdullaah al-Imaam- Muharram 25, 1428

The First Campaign:

The Warfare of Speech & Pen

This campaign against the *hijaab* attacks it with speech and by the pen- and its motive is the destruction of the woman. This is the mother of the campaigns, wherein they gather the multitudes to their call. They recruit and gather their means and tools, spend freely from their valuable wealth, and spend the best of their years carrying it out. They persist for decades in stirring up this campaign. They employ in this campaign of theirs these many doubts and misconceptions which are cast upon the Muslims, male and female, for the purpose of eradicating the love and preservation of the *hijaab* from the hearts of the Muslims as well as from their lives. And from these doubts and misconceptions:

The First Doubt or Misconception:

The saying of the callers to the destruction of the woman: **"We need to set the Muslim woman free from the heavy bonds placed upon her from the hijaab and other than it."**

The answer: This misconception is so widespread that there is no real need to mention the names of those who say it. It has become a slogan for them which they pride themselves on, and because of it they became stubborn and opinionated.

And the Islamic scholars have already confronted the people of this misconception. They have made clear that their saying this is due to the disease of their blind following of the enemies of Islaam. This is because the enemies of Islaam call to this "freedom". And how truthful is the speech of the Messenger, praise and salutations be upon him, concerning them:

31

{*"You will follow the example of those that came before you, hand span by hand span, arm span by arm span, until if they entered a lizard hole you would follow them." We said: Oh Messenger of Allaah, the Jews and the Christians? He said, "Who else?"*} (Narrated by al-Bukhaaree, Number 3456, and Muslim, Number 2669, and it is his wording, on Abi Sa'eed)

And the Muslim scholars say: From what is known to be certain, is that Islaam freed the Muslim woman from the time of ignorance. However, those who call for freeing her from that which is obligatory upon her from the *Shari'ah* (Islamic legislation) concerning the *hijaab* and other that it, turn away from the *Shari'ah* rulings, and they are accusing Allaah, the Most Kind, the All Aware with oppressing women, and Allaah is above that.

They also call to freeing the woman though they have no power to free her, since the One who does have that power is He who created her, and the Arranger of her affairs, and He who is in a position to guide her. For they are callers to a matter over which they have no power, and they are contenders with Allaah in that matter which He made specific for Himself Alone - legislating human affairs.

And it is said to them: Why is it that she cannot be freed except by removing her *hijaab*, and falling into going out beautified, and she cannot be freed if she chooses adherence to her *hijaab*, and the Islamic rules of conduct?!

Does not this "freedom" of theirs show that they need her to remain within reach of their hands in order to exploit her? And these are the deeds of the wolves of exploitation among the human race.

And the scholars say to them: Your condition of striving with all that is available to you to prevent the woman who wears *hijaab* from wearing her *hijaab*, and preventing the one who wants to wear the *hijaab* from doing so, has in fact stolen the freedom of the woman. And it has been made clear by this that you are truly the enemies of true freedom, and are frauds propagating a false freedom.

And they say to them also: The Muslim woman has not complained to you about that which you allege is her oppressed state, and she has not made you responsible for her; so why do you enter into her affairs, and afflict her, as well as her family and society, with different types of afflictions, and force her towards destruction? So what is this from you except that you violate her freedom and join her to that which you yourselves seek, by a path of treachery and deception in dealing with her?

And the scholars also say to them: You are transgressing into the place of the men (of her family). For there is no woman except that she has those whom she cannot marry amongst the men, and her close relatives who defend her, and her in-laws, so how do you transgress their rights and you say that you are freeing their women?!?

The Second Doubt and Misconception:

They say:

"There is no proof to be found in the Qur'aan concerning the hijaab"

The answer: This doubt is a widespread rumor from them, and I intend to mention here two sayings from the most famous callers to removing the Muslim women's *hijaab*.

As for the first: He is Husain ibn Ahmad Ameen, and he has said, "*I have reached the conclusion that the women's hijaab is not from Islaam.*"

And he has also said, "*There is not an ayat (verse in the Qur'aan) connecting the hijaab to Islaam.*"

We are quoting from the book, *"'Awdatu al-Hijaab"*, 1/268 (Compiler's Note: The Sheikh uses this as a reference in very specific context. So the reader should note that evidenced observations have been made regarding the author by the people of knowledge. And Allaah knows best.)

And as for the second: She is Nawaal As-Sa'daawee, and she has said that she is from a religious family, and she has read the Qur'aan forty times, and she has never found in it that which establishes the *hijaab*. (Quoted from the book, *"Lakay la Yatanaathir al-'Aqd"*)

The answer: This saying from them does not result from their ignorance of the verses that indicate the *hijaab*, because their presence is a known fact to the Muslims in general, except he whom Allaah has led astray. Rather, they result from astonishing boldness, dubious obstinacy, and strong resistance, and fabricating against Allaah and His Messenger, may Allaah's praise and His salutations be upon him. This eliminates trust in their sayings, and confidence in their research.

The Muslims have sure knowledge that the various evidences concerning the legislation of the *hijaab*, its obligation, and the necessity of it, as well as the proofs forbidding appearing beautified and adorned before strange men and the uncovering of the face are indeed many.

From them is the saying of the Most High, ﴾ *O Prophet! Tell your wives and your daughters and the women of the believers to draw their cloaks (veils) all over their bodies. That will be better, that they should be known (as free respectable women) so as not to be harassed. And Allaah is Ever Oft-Forgiving, Most Merciful.*﴿ -(Surat al-Ahzaab, Ayat 59)

And the Most High says ﴾ *...and to draw their veils all over juyubihinna (i.e. their bodies, faces, necks and bosoms, etc.)...*﴿ -(Surat an-Noor, Ayat 31)

And the Most High says, ﴾ *...and do not display yourselves like that of the times of ignorance...*﴿ -(Surah al-Ahzaab, Ayat 33)

And the Most High says, ﴾ *...And when you ask (his wives) for anything you want, ask them from behind a screen, that is purer for your hearts and for their hearts.*﴿ -(Surah al-Ahzaab, Ayat 53)

And the Most High says, ﴾ *And as for women past child-bearing who do not expect marriage, it is no sin on them if they discard their (outer) clothing in such a way as not to show their adornment. But to refrain (i.e. not to discard their outer clothing) is better for them. And Allaah is All-Hearer, All-Knower.*﴿ -(Surah an-Noor, Ayat 60)

And the proofs from the Sunnah concerning the *hijaab* are many also, and from them is that which comes in al-Bukhaaree, number 1652, and other than it from the hadeeth of Hafsah wherein she says, {*We used to treat the wounded from jihaad and look after the ill. Once my sister asked the Prophet, 'Is there any harm for any of us to not go out if she does not have an outer garment to cover her (jilbaab)?' He said, Her friend should dress her from her own jilbaabs, and she should participate in the good deeds and in the religious gathering of the Muslims }* "

And 'Aishah, may Allaah be pleased with her, she said that *{ Aflah, the brother Abu al-Qu'ays, sought permission to visit her- and he was her uncle by the nursing relationship-after the verses of the hijaab were revealed. She said, So I refused to give him permission. When Allaah's Messenger, praise and salutations be upon him, came, I told him about what I had done, and he ordered me to permit him to enter.} And in a narration he (Aflah), said to her, "Do you veil yourself from me and I am your paternal uncle?" And in a narration in Muslim, "And he was Abu al-Qu'ays, the husband of a woman who nursed 'Aishah."}* (The hadeeth is narrated in al-Bukhaaree, number 5103 and Muslim, number 1445)

And whoever wants further proofs concerning the *hijaab*, should consult our treatise, "*The Numerous Mistakes in the Pilgrimage of the Uncovered Woman*", for we brought all the proofs in detail there.

And they cannot deny the proofs of the *hijaab*, except that they are then like those who deny the existence of the sun on a cloudless sky during the last fourth of the day! They should know that by their saying this they are deviating from the majority of the Muslims.

The Third Doubt or Misconception:

Their saying:

"The Imaams agree that the face and hands are both excluded by the exception found in the saying of the Most High: ⦃ ... and not to show off their adornment except only that which is apparent...⦄-(Surat an-Noor, Ayat 31)

I say: that this is a well-known misconception from them, as Qaasim Ameen, the author of the book, *"Tahrir al-Mara'a"*, said, *"And the Imaams all agree that the face and the hands are from that which is excepted in the verse..."* (Quoted from the book, *"Awdatu al-Hijaab"*, (1/41))

The one who wrote the introduction of the previously mentioned source (1/53) said, criticizing these words of the said Qaasim, *"Qaasim relies upon the opinion of some of the legal scholars in allowing the uncovering of the face and the hands and feet, despite the fact that the opinion of those legal scholars in this permission is specific to the prayer only, not the issue of the hijaab and unveiling the face."*

I say: The people of knowledge agree upon the permissibility of the women uncovering her face and hands, however this is in the prayer, without the presence of strange men, as Sheikh al-Islaam Ibn Taymiyyah says, as recorded in *"Majmoo' al-Fataawa"* (22/115). He speaks about the *jilbaab* (the overgarment) in the prayer of the women: It is verified in the texts and the consensus of the legal scholars that it is not upon her in the *salaat* to wear the *jilbaab* which covers her if she is in her house; however, that the *jilbaab* is for if she goes out. At the time when she prays in her house, her face, hands, and feet can be seen.

As for that which is related to the exception stated in the verse, then it is authentically narrated on Ibn Mas'ood, as found in al-Haakim, and Ibn Abi Shaybah, and Ibn Jareer at-Tabari (19/155) that what is intended by it is the garments, not the face.

And it is related on Ibn 'Abaas as found in Ibn Abi Haatim in his *Tafseer* (8/6574) that he explained the exception as the face and the hands, and the strongest conclusion is that it is a weak unaccepted report in terms of the sciences of hadeeth.

Yet this weakly transmitted explanation of Ibn 'Abaas is used as a support for those who say that the exception in the verse is the face and the hands. While that which is authentically narrated upon him concerning the verses of the *hijaab* is that he said, "*She lowers the jilbaab over her face, and does not discard it.*" And this narration is in "*Masaa'il Abi Daawood Lee Ahmad*" (pages 104-155).

And what is evident is that the verse does not support the explanation of the exception of the face, because Allaah says, ⦃*...except only that which is apparent...*⦄-(Surat al-Ahzaab, 59). And ⦃ *that which is apparent* ⦄ is that which is revealed on its own, and not that which is made apparent deliberately by the woman, such as the face and the hands, because a woman deliberately displays the face or does not display it. And the explanation that is strongest concerning the verse is that which Ibn Mas'ood said, and many of the explainers of the Qur'aan state this along with him.

Indeed, the sayings of the consensus of the people of knowledge are plentiful concerning the continuity of the Muslim women covering themselves; and the covering of her face when she goes out amongst strangers, except during the major and minor pilgrimages.

In what follows, I mention from the sayings of the consensus of the scholars (concerning the obligation of covering the face), organizing them by their era.

Ibn al-Mundhir who died in the year 318 *Hijri*
Ibn 'Abdul-bar, who died in the year 423 *Hijri*, in *"at-Tamheed"* (15/108) and in *"al-Istidhkaar"*
Ibn Habeerah, who died in the year 520 *Hijri*, in his book *"al-Eedaah"* (1/284)
Ibn Rushd al-Hafeed, the year 595 *Hijri* in, *"Badaayat al-Mujtahid"* (1/332)
Ibn Qudaamah, who died in the year 620, in *"al-Mughni"* (5/154)
Abu al-Hasan Ibn al-Qataan, who died in the year 727 *Hijri*, in *"al-Iqnaa'"* (1/262) Number 1458
Ibn Taymeeyah, who died in the year 727 *Hijri*, as related in *"Majmoo' al-Fataawa"* (26/112)
Ibn Qayyim, who died in the year 752 *Hijri*, in *"Badaai' al-Fawaaid"* (3/141)
Ibn Muflah, who died in the year 763 *Hijri*, in *"al-Faroo'"* (3/450)
Ibn Raslaan, who died in the year 844 *Hijri*, quoted by ash-Shawkaanee in *"Nayl al-Awtaar"* (2/130)
Ibn Hajr, who died in the year 852 *Hijri*, in *"al-Fath"* (4/45)…and other than them.

And as for our time, then the statements of the people of knowledge concerning the obligation upon the woman to cover her face with the legislated *hijaab* are many, due to the fact that they are confronting the call for the Muslim women to uncover.

The Fourth Doubt or Misconception:

Their saying:

"Indeed the scholars differ regarding the covering of the face. As long as the scholars do not agree on the veiling of the face then the woman can uncover it and there is no sin upon her."

I say: The scholars of Islaam are agreed that it is obligatory for the Muslim woman to cover her face whenever there is fear of *fitnah* (trial, tribulation); and what age is greater in *fitnah* of the uncovered women, and the extensive call to that, than our time?! Such that the beautiful adorned women become commercialized throughout the world, and themselves become callers to that which the secularists want concerning the removal of the Islamic *hijaab* and other than it.

And also, it has not taken place- in any age from the preceding ages of the Muslims- that the callers to corruption on the earth have reached out to corrupt the Muslim woman through the removal of her *hijaab*, involving her in appearing adorned or improperly covered, as well as intermixing with the men. For this phenomenon has only occurred in our time- while none of the scholars have made it permissible.

Additionally, the evil call to this way of leaving the house adorned or improperly covered is not limited to uncovering the face only; rather, what follows after that is uncovering the head, and the throat, and the chest, and the shin; indeed even the thigh, because they want the Muslim women upon a contemptible show of nudity. Allaah curse them, how they lie! Also, those scholars who say that it is permissible for the women to uncover her face amongst strangers additionally say that in general, it is better for her to wear the veil as a protection from possible *fitnah*. As for when there clearly is *fitnah*, then they say that it is obligatory to do so.

Likewise, those scholars who said that uncovering the face is permissible in accordance with the preceding guidelines did not practically implement this call to uncover. Rather, they left the existing practice of the women in their adherence to the full body covering *hijaab*. Their difference merely was stated within their books, while the women of their family continued to adhere to the legislated *hijaab*. As for the corrupt callers who utilize the words of the people of knowledge as proof that it is permissible for the woman to uncover her face among strange men- then in reality they only make her a commodity, one which they market to the disbelieving countries. But what they achieve with this is a losing bargain, and they only achieve through this the fulfillment of their own desires.

So what is with these deviants and their selectively using the words of the people of knowledge as proof?! In their general estimation they, the scholars, are actually frauds, both worthless and insignificant. Indeed, the people of knowledge are considered enemies to them, as they judge that they are oppressors, backward, and that there is no true need in the Muslim nation for them, and that it is necessary to 'fling them into the sea'.

The Fifth Doubt or Misconception:

Their saying:

"Certainly the hijaab is from the ignorant customs, which the later day people only adopted from previous Muslims who were inflexible and strict."
(Quoted from the book, *"'Awdat al-Hijaab"* (1/19))

The answer: The falseness of this misconception is so clear that it really needs no mention , because the one who made the *hijaab* obligatory is Allaah, in His Book, and His Messenger, in his Sunnah. Then the Companions followed upon that, as well as the generation who followed them, and the generation who followed them, and the Muslims from after them, all the way up until our time.

Abu 'Ubaid al-Qaasim ibn Salaam al-Harawee, who died in the year 224 *Hijri*, said in *"Ghareeb al-Hadeeth"* (4/317-318), speaking about the saying of Allaah, the Most High, ⁅*...except only that which is apparent...*⁆-(Surat al-Ahzaab, 59), *"And that which is correct to be acted upon in our view is that narration from 'Abdullaah ibn Mas'ood related from Abi al-Ahwas, on 'Abdullaah ibn Mas'ood, that he said: "It means the garments."* Abu 'Abdullaah said, *"Meaning: Nothing is displayed from her beauty except the outer garment." "*

And Abu Hayaan said in his *tafseer,* "*He commanded the women to differ in their dress from the slave women, by wearing the outer robe, and coverings, and covering the heads, and the faces, to be modest and respected, such that there is no allure in them... and this is the custom of the country of Andaloos (present day Spain), where there is not displayed anything of the woman except her one eye.*"

Abu Haamid al-Ghazaalee said, *"Through the passing of the ages the men continue to uncover their faces, and the women to go out veiled."*

And al-Haafidh ibn Hajar said, in *"Fath al-Baaree"*, (9/405), *"And the custom of the women in the past and the women of today is still that they cover their faces amongst the men who it is impermissible for them to marry."*

Sheikh al-Islaam ibn Taymiyyah said, as found in *"Majmoo' al-Fataawa"* (15/372), *"It was the Sunnah of the believers in the time of the Prophet and his khulafaa (those who ruled after him) that the free woman veiled herself."*
And al-'Aynee, and al-Qistalaanee, and al-Mubaarakafooree, as well as others, state something similar to this.

The Sixth Doubt or Misconception:

Their saying:

"The hijaab is simply a custom whose use is not appropriate in our time."

Qaasim Ameen states this misconception in his book, *"al-Mara'at al-Jadeedah"*, page 18, and we quote it from *"'Awdatu al-Hijaab"* (1/66). Some of them state a more explicit statement, as they say, *"The hijaab was only in the time of oppression."*

The answer: This misconception indicates the greatness of the speaker's fascination with that which the disbelievers have of worldly desires, and the prevalence of depravity and licentiousness among them. We know of many from those who go to the lands of the disbelievers- to study in them, like Qaasim Ameen- who return and they do not know anything from Islaam at all; indeed some of them return and they disapprove of and find every good thing something repulsive, and praise what those disbelievers have of immorality and decadence. This is because their hearts absorb what is spewed out by the intellects of the disbelieving intellectuals, which they feel is superior to the way of the Muslims. It is not strange that they find the truth as bitter, as they see good as evil, obscenity and corruption as progress, and uprightness as backwardness. Their state of mind is corrupted and their intellects contaminated, and their innate character becomes soiled.

And who is more worthy than them of applying the saying of Allaah upon them, Most High, ﴾ *And when it is said to them, "Make not mischief on the earth," they say," We are only peacemakers. Verily, they are the ones who make mischief, but they perceive not.*﴿-(Surat al-Baqara, Ayats 11-12)

The Seventh Doubt or Misconception:

Their saying about the Muslims:

"The hijaab is a custom that came to them through associating with some outside nations. The Muslims approved of it, took hold of it, and exaggerated in it. Then they dressed it in the clothes of the religion, as they have done with other harmful customs which become established amongst the people in the name of religion, while the religion is free from them."

(Quoted from the book mentioned earlier, *"Awdatu al-Hijaab"* (1/41))

I say: They mean by "The people who the Muslims associate and mix with" -the Magians, the Jews, the Christians, and the Berbers. Some of them state clearly that the Muslims took the *hijaab* from the Persians. The fraud, Husayn ibn Ahmad Ameen, says, *"And from what is known is that the first commentators on the Noble Qur'aan without exception were from the Persians. And it is natural for the commentators to be influenced by the customs and those established behaviors which originate from the elite, who were socially above them."*

This is a clear falsehood, an obvious, absurd contention, and in hopeless opposition to the truth. It is a case of shamefully fabricating lies on Allaah and His Messenger, may Allaah's praise and salutations be upon him, and on the Muslims. Indeed there is in the Noble Qur'aan more than one verse in which the *hijaab* is mentioned, and likewise in the pure authentic Sunnah. Also, when did the Magians and the Berbers have *hijaab*?!? As for the Jews and the Christians, the *hijaab* was made obligatory in their religious laws, except that they have changed and modified these laws; and many from them have not preserved the *hijaab* in practice.

They take this false doubt from the Orientalists. They suppose that it will be enthusiastically accepted among the Muslims, yet they are surprised that the Muslims see it as the utmost falsehood.

The Eighth Doubt or Misconception:

Their saying:
"That which we see today widespread amongst the young women and the ladies from that which is called "The Islamic Dress"; Islaam is free from it, as it is an exact imitation of the attire of the Christian nuns. We all know that there is no priesthood or monasticism in Islaam."
(Quoted from the preceding source (1/128))

I say: Certainly they cast at the Muslim woman who wears *hijaab* every possible rock and clod of mud, and portray her as having every evil and trouble. Their overwhelming rancor towards the *hijaab* has blinded them from contemplating what they say. For when does the woman who is adhering to her religion need that which the nuns have, after Allaah has enriched her with Islaam?! How can they claim this is true, when it is known with certainty that the Muslim women were instructed in the *hijaab* by Allaah, the Omniscient, the All-Knowing, in His book, and His, the Most Compassionate, the Most Merciful, Messenger, may Allaah's praise and salutations be upon him, in his Sunnah?! Therefore their statement is nothing but an example of falsehood.

More than one of the scholars has stated that Allaah made the *hijaab* obligatory upon the women of Bani Israa'eel, so if the nuns wear *hijaab*, then that is only that previous command, which agrees with our revealed *Shari'ah*.

The Ninth Doubt or Misconception:

Their saying:

"Indeed the Muslims are petty, because they reduce Islaam to only being one piece of cloth; and it is "al-hijaab". They raise a clamor about it without justification, and they inflame the world, occupying the people from important issues."
(Quoted from the book, *"at-Tararif al-'Almaanee fee Mawaajihah"* page 100)

The answer: The fickle cling to moss, as the saying goes. In the above statement they make the *hijaab* into something insignificant, while in most of their speech the *hijaab* is a towering cliff in front of them, and blocking of their progress.

I say to them: If the *hijaab* to you is an insignificant thing, then why have you come out in force against it, and why do you ask for help from the various nations and the political parties in fighting, combating, and eradicating it? And why do you attack the Muslim women who wear the *hijaab*? And why do you eventually come to remove the *hijaab* of some of those who answer your call? You thought that *hijaab* had vanished forever, and then it quickly returned. Is this proof that it is insignificant and unwanted, or proof that it is significant, and that which the woman has a natural disposition for?!

We know that they fight against the *hijaab* after they have studied aspects of its status and role, such as the wisdom behind its legislation, and its obligation, and the reality of the Muslim women's adherence to it throughout the ages of history. They necessarily have drawn the conclusion that *hijaab* is a sign of distinction, and modesty, and chastity, and an invitation to virtue. Similarly, they see that the women who wear the *hijaab* do not accept their call to uncover their faces, and to immorality and degradation. For if the *hijaab* is no more than a piece of cloth, as the author quoted previously says, then its people (that is, the ones who oppose the *hijaab*) are like the insane, engaging in a battle in which they have no adversaries; but rather the truth is that they see that the *hijaab* prevents them from spreading that which they aim for concerning tribulations and corruption, as well as the spreading of practices of vice and depravity.

The Tenth Doubt or Misconception:

Their saying:
"The hijaab is offensive to others."
(Quoted from the book, *"at-Tatarif al-'Almaanee..."* page 109)

I say: They mean by "offensive" that the *hijaab* is only a traditional garment, or a distinguishing feature of certain sects; and this is not true. And if they were just in their statement concerning the *hijaab*, they would say: "In it is the preservation of the rights of others." Do they not see that the woman who does not wear the *hijaab* causes people to become enamored with her, so she corrupts the affection and love that exists between men and their wives? On the other hand, the woman who wears the *hijaab* is a preserver of this familial affection, love, and mercy. Also, the woman who is uncovered causes quarrels and conflict between the people; even fighting in some circumstances. The woman who wears *hijaab* does not cause anything from this.

The Eleventh Doubt or Misconception:

Their saying:
"The hijaab is a symbol of severity and extremism."
(Quoted from the book, *"at-Tatarif al-'Almaanee..."*)

The answer: How free is Allaah from all imperfections! This is a great slander, and a twisting of the truth. If the *hijaab* indicates that the woman is obedient to her Lord, preserving of her modesty, safeguarding her honor, and has a vigilant concern for her chasteness- then is this extremism and severity, or is it moderation and temperance?! There is no doubt that it is in fact moderation and temperateness, though they falsely insist that it is strictness and extremism.

Indeed, we say to them: Show us the moderates who stand with you? For you do not find them praising any from amongst the women except she who extends her hand to them, and who becomes submissive to them in carrying out their desires and wishes. Indeed the woman who does not accept that which they are proposing, she is "too strict", even if she is one who does not veil herself. So it is said to them: Indeed, you are truly the inflexible ones, because you impose upon the woman that which is not acceptable intellectually or by natural disposition. As how can this be acceptable, if it differs with Allaah's laws?

The Twelfth Doubt or Misconception:

Their saying:

"The woman who wears the hijaab is unable to carry out her work outside her house."

The response: This doubt is the droning on of those who contend that they are seeking to rectify the economic condition of the woman. From the first of those who transmitted it into the ears of the people, is the tyrant Jamaal 'Abdun-Naasir, the former leader of the Egyptian Arab Republic.

And this speech is from the arsenal of those who are enamored with the Western ideal, for when has the Muslim woman ever complained to them of this? Indeed history confirms that the woman who wore the *hijaab* performed her work outside of her house, in that which was harder than the modern jobs today, for she was able- and still is- to work on the farms, and gather wood, and other than that, and she still preserved her *hijaab*. Conversely, her going out beautified and adorned actually hinders her from performing her work well, and starting it promptly, because if the woman who wears the *hijaab* wishes to go out quickly, she puts on her *hijaab* and goes out. This differs from the one who beautifies herself to go out, as she requires time in order to beautify herself for the men, and clothe herself in what is agreeable to them. Also, the woman who goes out beautified is not able to perform the jobs that the woman who wears *hijaab* is able to perform, because she needs to keep acting as those who are present desire. Indeed she may flirt with her body at times, and looks to the right sometimes, and to the left at other times, in order to impress

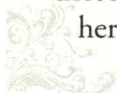

whoever is looking at her. She may not take her work seriously, and falls short in it, because she is preoccupied with the ends which they desire.

We expound upon this in our book, *"al-Mu'aamrat al-Kubra 'ala al-Marat al-Muslimah";* that if the woman is required to work outside her house, she must remain in compliance with the conditions of Islamic law. And from that: Her work must be far removed from any intermixing with the men.

The Thirteenth Doubt or Misconception:

Their saying:
"The hijaab is a cause for the decline of the Muslims, for they cannot progress except through its removal."

The response: This is a prevailing claim amongst these callers, as it even reaches the tongues of their poets. Their poet, the corrupt deviant Jameel Sadeeqee az-Zahaawee in his collection of poems wrote:

> *"The Muslims are held back from the nations of the earth*
> *The hijaab makes the Muslim women miserable."*

At first, this claim was enthusiastically received by those who were misled by their propaganda, and who were deceived by their slogans. As for the rational ones, then they knew from the start that it was a scheme and deception. As for the woman who accepts this claim, and who has for awhile been working and looking to advance herself, it becomes clear to her and to all of those who are able to hear and see and understand that this alleged "progress" never materializes. On the contrary, what occurs is that the woman becomes unhappy, and those who are connected with her also become unhappy, and she openly admits this. Despite the voices being raised, and the slogans increasing, the woman who is in competition with men has not progressed in a way of honor for her, or respect. Rather, she has become exposed to violation, and heard with her ears that which the callers to progress are saying: "*Indeed, the progressive woman is everyone's woman.*" Such that fear and dismay descend suddenly upon her. So where is the progress for the one who is in this condition?!

Additionally, economically there is no progress: Indeed she begins to spend a great deal of her wealth in purchasing different types of adornments, in order to please her employers, and what is left is wasted on travelling and other pursuits. Thus she does not benefit from it but a little, and the extent that she is damaged by its evil is disastrous. And as for falling behind on fulfilling her husband's rights, and her children's rights- their performance is lost, and this is something that has become accepted and normal. As for her disobedience to her Lord, and her opposition to her Messenger, may Allaah's praise and salutations be upon him, then what is more significant than that?

The Fourteenth Doubt or Misconception:

Their saying:

"That which prohibits the woman who wears hijaab from beautifying herself to go out is that she lacks the ability to purchase expensive dresses, and stylish garments."
(Refer to the book that was previously mentioned, *"Awdatu al-Hijaab"* (1/127))

I say: They don't know what they're talking about! They are referring to that which is not a legitimate criticism from the start, such as this saying of theirs; so what is their position concerning the wealth that is possessed by many of the Muslims?! Rather, there are indeed those who are affluent, and they are numerous. Do they still adhere to the *hijaab* because they only have a small amount of wealth?!

To summarize: The goal of those who dishonor both the *hijaab* and those Muslim women who adhere to it, is to eradicate from the minds of the Muslims the fact that preservation of the *hijaab* is a matter whose source is faith, chastity, truthfulness and sincerity.

I have found it sufficient to mention what has proceeded, from the doubts and misconceptions, without mentioning some others, because this is evidence as to their being plentiful. The reason there are so many of them is their desire to influence the general Muslims, men and women, by them, in their various conditions and states. This is proof of their efforts to expand the campaign of argumentation and deception regarding *hijaab*. Their purpose is to persuade the Muslims to answer their hopeless call to remove the *hijaab,* and cease wearing the *hijaab*- but this is impossible. It is impossible for them to achieve that, for Allaah is victorious in His command, but most of mankind do not know.

From the Effects of this Campaign:

From the effects of this campaign is that the hijaab was limited to covering the head and the neck, not the face.

And from that which has falsely became known as "legislated *hijaab*", is the woman simply covering her head and neck, while uncovering her face, and this is NOT called *hijaab* according to what which Allaah has legislated. This is because it conflicts with the stated proofs concerning the obligation of the *hijaab* and its realization; and its form is covering the whole of the woman's body, including her face and hands.

We have mentioned the proofs that the legislated *hijaab*- rather, the obligatory *hijaab*- includes the woman covering her face and hands, in the refutation of the doubts mentioned in this campaign.

The result is that this devised concept of the *hijaab* which has been mentioned is put forward as a substitute for the true form of legislated *hijaab*. And the campaign is now directed towards the one who suffices with this "*hijaab*", as has occurred in Turkey and other than it.

Look at how much the woman who is satisfied with the mentioned misconception of "*hijaab*" must endure, having left the legislated *hijaab*. Now she is no longer protected from harm. She is not of those who strictly comply with the legislated *hijaab*, as her persistence in wearing the mentioned "*hijaab*" is her battle against the legislated *hijaab*, even if she does not intend that. With the passage of time the result will be no true *hijaab*, except this new form which they have become acquainted with, and there is no strength nor power except with Allaah.

The Second Campaign:

The Campaign whose Weapon is Force Against the Hijaab & Those who Adhere

to it

*W*hen the secularists and those similar to them from the people of corruption in the land of the Muslims saw that the *hijaab* will never be removed, and the weapons of the first campaign had not had any significant effect, they turned to the enactment of laws which give them the authority to use force and degradation against the one who is wearing the *hijaab*. And the first to use violence against the Muslim women who wore *hijaab* was the tyrant, the Pharoah of Turkey, Mustafa Kamaal Ataaturk, the demolisher of the Uthmaani caliphate.

The previously mentioned author says in his book, *"Awdatu al-Hijaab"* 1/205: *"As for the removal of the hijaab of the Turkish women, it was accomplished through intimidation and physical infringements, as the police carried out the removal of the Turkish women's hijaab with force."*

The author of the treatise, *"at-Tatarif al-'Almaanee fee Mawaajihatu al-Hijaab"*, said, on page 25, *"The most dangerous of the poisoned arrows which Ataaturk was to aim towards the throat of the Muslim woman was his decree in the end of the year 1926 which came about due to his objective of prohibiting women from wearing hijaab. He made it obligatory upon them to uncover their faces. In addition, the Turkish parliament issued a command prohibiting the women from wearing the jilbaab, or outer garment, and making it compulsory for them to wear only a dress; otherwise their husbands and family members would be brought to trial."*

I say: It is not strange that the tyrant Ataaturk recruited the police to confront the Muslim women, as he was from the most extreme of the apostates. It has been related from him that he said, speaking to the Muslims of Turkey, *"You will never be successful as long as this shabby Qur'aan is in front of you"* Then he threw a copy of the Arabic

Qur'aan. So Allaah will pay him back with that which he deserves!

He also said, addressing the speaker, Ellison, *"You are talking about the religion; so know then that I am a man without a religion. How pleased I would be if it was in my power to cast the religions, in their entirety, into the sea. The ruler who feels in need of religion in order to support this government, then he has an ignorant perspective and weak authority. He attempts to control the citizens with a fragile rope."* (Quoted from the book *"Awdatu al-Hijaab"* referred to previously (1/209))

The author of the treatise *"at-Tatarif al-'Almaanee..."* says on page 19 that Mustafa Ataaturk said, *"We are now in the twentieth century, and we do not need to follow behind a Book which discusses the fig and the olive."* Here the Jews applauded saying in support of him, *"We delivered the country to Ataaturk, and we left the Ka'bah to the Arabs."*

And these bold secularists continue in their war against the *hijaab*, emulating the oppressor Ataaturk.

From them: The Shah, Ridaa Bahluli, the leader of the Iranian state in that time. Muhammad ibn Ahmad Ismaa'eel said in his book, *"Awdatu al-Hijaab"* (1/215), *"When the English colonials installed Ridaa Bahluli as Shah of Iraan in the year 1926, establishing the Bahluli family, he immediately abolished the legislated hijaab, and his wife was the first to uncover her face in an official ceremony. Then his command was issued to the police to harass the women who refused to follow the example of their queen, and went out wearing the hijaab. No woman left her home veiled, except that she returned unveiled, as the police would remove her hijaab by force, and confiscate her abaya (her Islamic overgarment), and treat its wearer, as much as possible, in a contemptible, degrading manner . He prohibited the young women and the teachers from wearing the hijaab and going to their schools with it. He forbade any officer from the army officers from appearing in public places, or in the street with a woman wearing hijaab, regardless of how she was connected or related to him. Ridaa Khan was an intimate friend of Kamaal Ataaturk, and he always persisted in blindly following him, and in following after him step by step. In his actions, Ridaa Bahluli imitated exactly Ataaturk, the original, in his war on Islaam.*" It was also stated, in the same source (1/215): "*And in Afghanistaan the authorities in charge removed the hijaab with legislation, and that was in the era of Muhammad Amaan.*"

The preceding author also said in the same source, page 217, "*And in Tunisia Boorkeebah called for the liberation of the women from the "shackles" of the religion, and made her a vehicle for his secular ideology. In a speech of Habeeb Boorkeebah in "Pyramids". 12/20/1975, the president of Tunisia announced that he established legislation, in the year 1956, prohibiting the marrying of more than one wife. He considered the marrying of more than one wife to be an offense whose perpetrator would be punished with imprisonment for the period of a year, as well as a monetary fine of 240 dinaars.*"

I say: When the tyrant "liberates the women from the shackles of the religion" he first destroys the *hijaab*. After Boorkeebah was himself ruined, another leader, Zayn al-'Aabideen ibn 'Alee, came after him, and he proceeded forward with the same secular ideology. From this was a war on the *hijaab*, which he deemed to be a sectarian or divisive garment. The women who wore *hijaab* were treated in a way in which they never treated the enemies of Islaam!

The author previously mentioned also said, in the same source, "*In Somalia the government of Seeaad Buray was strong in its assault against Islaam in Somalia. They recently expelled every student who wore Islamic apparel from the schools, as well as abolishing the explanation of the Noble Qur'aan from their curriculum. They began to expel the students who were discovered performing the prayer, or were reading the Noble Qur'aan, from the schools.*"

He also said, as stated in the preceding source (1/216), "*In Algeria Ahmad ibn Baylaa stole the Islamic revolution, and changed it into a socialist revolution which was far removed from Islaam and opposed to it. He used a strange argument to call the Algerian women to remove the hijaab. He said, 'Certainly the Algerian women refrained from taking off the hijaab in the past, because France was the one who called her to do so. As for today, then I call upon the Algerian woman to remove her hijaab for the sake of her country, Algeria.'*"

He also stated in the previously mentioned book (1/218), "*In Egypt 'Abdun-Nasr and his enforcers and goons authored a book, "al-Mithaaq" in which he followed the example of his first leader, Ghengis Khan, when the latter wrote his book, "al-Yaasiq" in order to turn the people away from the Qur'aan through it. From which is presented in respect to the women in "al-Mithaaq": 'The woman is equal to the man, and she must throw off the remaining shackles which hinder her move towards freedom until she is able to take part with the man wholeheartedly and positively in her position in life.'*"

I say: And from these "shackles"- in their view and perspective- is the *hijaab*.

The author of the treatise *"at-Tatarif al-'Almaanee fee Mawaajihatu al-Hijaab"*, page 111, said, *"Its beginning was in Turkey, "The Khalifah's Land", when Kamaal Ataaturk undertook the magnification of this issue. Then all of those who came after him from the secular governments followed his example, and tread upon his path; those who came to power in the Land of the Muslims, among them:*

Amaan Allaah Khan did that in the land of Afghaanistaan, as did Ridaa Bahluli in Iraan, and 'Abdun-Nasr in Egypt, and al-Habeeb Boorkeebah in Tunisia, and other than them from the secular governments; those who adopted the secularist ideal for their governments, and as a constitution for their lives. They adopted a way of governing which was emptied and drained of any Islamic sources or foundations, and pulled up its existing roots from the Muslim lands."

I say: The persecution of the governments of these countries, and those like them, towards the Muslim woman who wears *hijaab* has intensified, until it has even led to their expulsion, of which the author of the treatise, *"at-Tatarif al-'Almaanee fee Mawaajihatu al-Hijaab"*, page 31, says concerning them, *"However, the absolute secularists insist on expelling those women who wear hijaab, such that if she studies outside her land, then the high council of education mandates that acceptable qualifications are not based upon the diplomas granted by outside authorities, except if the student, male or female, also takes a required qualification test after he returns to his land. Then an obstacle is blatantly placed in front of the student who wears hijaab which is not in conformity with their regulations. As she is prohibited from taking the required exam unless she removes her hijaab."*

This degradation of the women wearing *hijaab* brings about various matters. We will summarize them in the following:

1. They violate the freedom of the people without any right to do so. This violation is a disgrace especially for them, as it shows the falseness and insincerity of their call to grant the people freedom. Also, their doing this shows that what they intend by freedom is removing the Muslims from practicing the Islamic legislation, whether the Muslims desire this or not.

2. The interfering and meddling of the secularists and those who support them, in the self determined affairs of the Muslims which are specific to those Muslims; those affairs which they have no right to enter into, such as the women's dress.

3. By this evil attack on the *hijaab* and those who adhere to it, the enemies of Islaam from the Jews and Christians achieve more than they dreamed of, and far above that which they are capable of achieving themselves, concerning the Muslim woman and her family. France, the mother of depravity, has issued a law prohibiting the women who wear *hijaab* from entering university halls, and from public occupations. As of yet it has not yet occurred that the *hijaab* has been prohibited entirely in France, meaning removed from every Muslim woman in the street and other than it. It is as if those from our countrymen say to their leaders from the Jews and the Christians: Increase in praise for us and rewards; and we will further increase in the subjugation and humbling of the Muslims.

4. It is apparent from this war on the *hijaab* and those who adhere to it: The reality of this war which is lead by the call to remove the *hijaab*, is actually warfare on Islaam in totality, not only the *hijaab*. This exposure of those people who are the "ideological students" of the Jews and Christians should awaken the Muslims, and make them see that the call to remove the *hijaab* will eventually lead them to turn away from Islaam, and to gradually approach the inferior practices and depravity of the disbelievers.

The Callers to Removal of the Hijaab Exploit the Rulers' Persecution of the Muslim Women to Dishonor the Hijaab and Do Away with it

That which the rulers engage in- except for those upon whom Allaah has mercy- in the judicial courts concerning the *hijaab* are like a dream come true to the callers to the corruption of the women.

They become a means for them to initiate the discarding of the *hijaab*, and its removal, in the plain sight and hearing of the people. The author of *"Awdatu al-Hijaab"* (1/241) says, when he summarizes an article from one of the criminals amongst the callers to liberation: "*The objective of this article (as can be derived from its wording and expressions) is to challenge the phenomenon of returning to the hijaab, and they advance the explicit call to remove the hijaab and cast it into the sea and drown it there, where it will become utterly forgotten. The result of this is the full imitation of the western woman in all that she does or does not do.*"

As for the female callers to discard the *hijaab*, then they have found in the alleged oppression of the women who wear *hijaab* an opportunity for themselves to cast off their own *hijaab* in the open sight and hearing of the Muslims.

The previously mentioned author mentioned in the book we have previously cited (1/109), footnote number 201, "*I have mentioned that Saafee Naaz Kaathim and Hudaa Sha'raawee and Seeza Nabaraawee threw off their hijaab and trampled it under their feet, upon participating in an international women's conference which met in Rome in the summer of 1923.*"

He also said in his book (1/246), when he was discussing one of the authors, "*The author entered into an inadequate comparison between "tonight" and "last night" in the life of the Egyptian women and the return to hijaab, and he said, May Allaah repay him as he deserves, "Is there nothing more distant than the difference in the life of the Egyptian woman between tonight and last night: as yesterday, she cast her hijaab into the sea, at the Alexandrian shore, announcing her entrance into the age of light. As for "tonight", then, by her own choice, she requests from the devils of darkness to weave for her a hijaab to repel her from the light of day.*"

The author of the book, *"Madha Yurideen min al-Mara'"*, pages 80-81, says, "*In one of the Gulf schools, called, Safiyyah bint 'Abd al-Mutalib School, may Allaah be pleased with her, they put together an activity which they then showed on the television. The mature young women danced covered, veiled, and continued in this dance until they progressively slipped off their abayas which had covered their faces and bodies; then at the end of the dance they threw them under their feet, and they began to dance in short dresses and exposed arms, their hair swaying right and left.*"

I say: And whoever from amongst them has never been able to cast aside the *hijaab* in her country, or among her family, then she does so when she goes to the lands of the disbelievers, because she does not want to proclaim and reflect the morals and ethics of her religion. In reality, she only wants to display that which those disbelievers are pleased with.

The author of the book, *"Lakay la Yatanaathir al-Aqd"* (pages 89-90) quoted, when discussing some of hypocrites of the *hijaab* who had stated "*I have been lead by love of the new, to be diverse in the way I wear (my hijaab). So at times you see me with it upon my shoulders, not on my head, in order to show off my beauty and something of my stylishness. Once when I travelled to a foreign country, I was not satisfied with merely beautifying my hijaab. Instead, I took it off and threw it in down on the airplane seat in which I was travelling.*"

The previously mentioned author, in his book, *"'Awdatu al-Hijaab"* (1/72), in a footnote, said, when discussing the visit of the then King of Afghanistan and his wife to Egypt, "*When the visit ended, and the Queen of Afghanistan ascended the gangplank onto the Italian steamship which was transporting her to Europe, she hastened to remove her hijaab in a gesture of group spirit. She said to the journalists, 'I think that we are not returning in shackles by the orders of King Fuwaad here.'*"

So these gestures pleasing to Shaaytan, from those who have been mentioned, have made a sound that is heard worldwide, and the newspapers for hire endorse and are pleased with the like of these actions. They are happy with these mercenaries who are sent by the enemies of Islaam, as they have achieved that which the Jews and the Christians clearly hope for. Yet Allaah is triumphant over His affairs, but most of the people do not know.

The Defense of the Scholars of Islaam, and the Callers to Allaah, and the Right-Minded Muslims of the Legislated Hijaab

Already the enthusiastic from the scholars of Islaam and the callers to it, and the intelligent Muslims, and their writers and their educators, have put forth an unparalleled defense of the *hijaab*, in prose and poetry, and authoring books. They brought forth a significant number of refutations of the book by Qaasim Ameen, *"Tahreer al-Mara'"*. Muhammad ibn Ismaaeel says in his book *"'Awdatu al-Hijaab"*, (1/50), "*The callers to the truth and the defenders of the hijaab were not satisfied with stern articles; instead they composed numerous books, which reached in number one hundred books. They invalidated the doubts raised by Qaasim and established the proof upon him from the pure Shari'ah evidences.*" He then mentioned a number of books and treatises written for that purpose.

Some of the callers to truth and defenders of the *hijaab* have adopted other techniques to suppress these transgressors against the *hijaab*. From these techniques is that which was mentioned by the author of the previously mentioned book, *"'Awdatu al-Hijaab"*, (1/73). While discussing Qaasim Ameen he says, "*From that which is narrated from an intimate friend of his (he is the Islamic historian Rafaaq al-'Athm), is that he visited him (Qaasim Ameen) once, and when he opened the door for him, he said to him, 'This time I have come in order to discuss some societal issues directly with your wife."* Qaasim Ameen was surprised: How does he his associate seek to speak directly to his wife, and have a discussion with her? So he (Rafaaq) said to his friend, "Isn't this what you call to?

How can you encourage others towards that which you do not accept in practice yourself?" So Qaasim Ameen fell silent, speechless."

From the most notable stances in the faces of the call to *tabaruj* and unveiling the face is that which the author of the book, *"Hijaab al-Mara'at al-Muslimah",* mentions on page 487. He says, while speaking of the naming of Sa'd Zaghlool as minister, that lady Faatimah 'Asmat said, *"A group of Egyptian women in Cairo wanted to meet with him (the new minister) concerning a certain issue. He was astounded when he entered the place they were and they were covering their faces with the hijaab. He then refused to enter except on the condition that they uncover their faces. However, they refused, so the meeting never took place."*

I mentioned in my book, *"al-Mu'aamirat liKubra 'ala al-Mara'at al-Muslimah",* a number of women who take a very strong stand against the removal of the *hijaab*.

As for poetry in defense of the *hijaab*, then there is very much. Ahmad Muhrim says:

Are you deluded, oh Asmaa, by what Qaasim believes?
I stand on this side of the curtain, for the man is mistaken
They cannot bear to be confined by the hijaab and what is with it
Except that which veils this view and claim
Security is found in the character of all the East
When I am not allowed in the honorable inner rooms

Qaasim do not strike with your army and your
people
> Islaam is that which comes from Allaah's
> knowledge

And for us through His book Allaah has established honor
> And it is always superior to the events and new ages

The veiled women are our concern and we wish them to be
> Separated, the way of life is safeguarded and is
> harmonious

And this man by night casts off his ewes
> To where they are pursued by the oppressive wolf

And every life blunts the display of disgrace
> Not like a life which is wrapped in wrongdoing

The ship does not soar on the air ascending
> If it rises above the doves' stars (Altair and Vega)

Allaah forgive the people who persist in their opinions
> For it is not the trustworthy way and not the steadfast
> view

Is not within Islaam the cure for the drunkard
> Truly the Book of Allaah has the definitive medicine.

Another poet attacked it, saying:

Indeed, the faces are beautiful without a veil
> They hunt the prey in a trap of the eyes

If a girl leaves the inner room unveiled
> She drives the one of intellect to insanity

And another statement condemning this call:

> Our Book and our Prophet prohibit unveiling
> So examine the narrations and the verses
> These faces are the gardens of which she is proud
> To the beholders of the beauty of the woman
> She was concealed in the veils, hidden
> Her virtue was guarded, it could not be touched
> Today desires have opened it so she has fallen into
> flirtation of glances and kisses
> Protect your beauty with the veil for indeed it is
> The concealment of beauty and the manifestation of good deeds

'Aishah at-Taymooriyah said, as collected in *"Awdat al-Hijaab"*, 1/149-150:

> With the chaste hand the honor of my hijaab is protected
> And with my virtue superior to my companions
> With thoughtfulness and brilliance and purity
> All this has completed my good manners
> It will not harm my character and my good upbringing
> Or my being one of the blossoms of intellect
> My modesty does not hinder me from my high endeavors
> and lowering the khimaar and veil over me does not bring misfortune

I say: My saying is that which your sister said before:

> Oh people rectify yourselves
>> Today the arrows of unveiling have failed
> My veil is the center and the border of my honor
>> I will never leave it even if I taste suffering

And guard against those:

> Who said: remove from yourself the hijaab
>> Or what do you need with this concealment
> Welcome the new era of unveiling
>> Today cast away the veil
> The age of hijaab has been dismantled
>> Its remaining days are limited, diminishing and vanishing

And dumbfound and silence their spokesmen saying:

> For I answered them and the laughter filled
>> my mouth and I did not hold back in my response
> Be careful! for this call that has
>> deceived you is nothing but a glittering mirage
> And does not the West see how
>> The men after it become like wolves
> Or do they not see that this nakedness
>> Splinters the morals into many fragments
>> How many glances at a face
>>> Bring them to an end of glowing fiery embers

If you truly wish for your women
To be protected and living contentedly
Then abandon unveiling for its corrupt people
And return your women to the veil

The Plan to Remove the Hijaab of the Muslim Woman Aspires to Connect the Muslim Woman to the Western Disbelieving Women

Perhaps the Muslims that hear the call to eliminate the Muslim women's *hijaab* think that it merely calls to uncover the face and hands, and that will be sufficient. However, they will be surprised to find that it is part of a series of schemes, and the call to abandon the *hijaab* is only the first phase of many that the Muslim woman is being targeted with. When some of the Muslim women remove their *hijaab*, the callers to remove the *hijaab* then unmask their fangs, and expose the bitter reality. The reality being the call to the Muslim woman to follow the disbelieving Western women, and that they take them as examples and models of reference. Following are some of their sayings that are proofs against them indicating this; and their actions, which expose them, further demonstrate this:

The previously mentioned author said in his book, *"'Awdat al-Hijaab"*, (1/115), discussing the caller to unveil and to improper *tabaruj*, Hudaa Sha'raawee, *"And in a speech which Hudaa delivered at an occasion to celebrate the twentieth anniversary of the women's union (that is, the day that Egypt was accepted as a member in the International Woman's Union), she said, " We make for ourselves a pledge to follow the example of our Western sisters in promoting our gender, whatever that requires, and that we honestly and sincerely take part in carrying out the program of the International Woman's Union, which includes our mutual goals."*

A weekly political newspaper wrote an article written about the young women of Turkey (1962), which portrays in it a steamship used by the Turkish Ministry of Trade as a public exhibition in a trip paid for by the government, which travelled with them to well-known European ports. The article said, *"This steamship carried twenty five of the young, new, Turkish women, all of whom were quite beautiful. They had their hair cut short, and there was no visual distinction between them and the young women from London and Paris." The reporter said, "Most of the young women are speaking English with surprising skill. Some of them are known to have gained this proficiency in American colleges in Constantinople."*

He related some of what the young women spoke publicly about. An example from what one of them said in some of the English ports is, *"Truly, today's Turkish woman is free, and will no longer travel the roads in oppression. We live today like your English women. We wear modern European and American clothing. We dance, smoke cigarettes, and travel, and we go about without our husbands."*

Another example of their statements is that their life on the deck of the steamship is a happy one, a happiness that cannot be described. They all dance, and at nightfall they begin to dance the Tango and Foxtrot. All dances learned in such foreign schools.

The newspaper reporter commented on that description, saying, "*This is of the clearest of signs, which proves the progress of the Turkish woman, and her keeping pace with her Western sisters in the field of work, as well as the ideological and economic struggle. Every Turkish patriot cannot but envy her this progress.*" Quoted from the preceding book, "*'Awdat al-Hijaab*" (1/207-208)

And following this is Dariyah Shafeeq, one of the callers to discard the *hijaab*. She says, as quoted in "*'Awdat al-Hijaab*", (1/123): "*In spite of the fact that most educated Egyptians are extremely influenced by the French culture, and in spite of the fact that much of the outward forms of our social life are taken from the outward form of French social life; we do not find in our present times an example superior to the English ideal, in whose footsteps we hope to proceed upon in our efforts as women, upon its example and guidance. We take the ideal of the ideal people, which is portrayed in the English lady, who follows the example of the Queen of England, as ideals. They are examples for us in our struggle, for the sake of the Egyptian woman and her share in the world.*"

Look, oh my sister, to this depravity that the one who accepts the call to liberation falls into, and to this questionable statement, and the appalling disfigurement of morals, and values, and the Islamic character- indeed, on the essence of Islaam. Look how these calamity-stricken callers aim at cutting off their connection to the mothers of the believers, the wives of the Messenger, may Allaah's praise and salutations be upon him, and may Allaah be pleased with all of them, and cutting off the connection with the women of the Companions, who were the best of the believing women, and from their Muslim sisters who are still adhering to Islaam. And they substitute that with following the modern examples of the unchaste, uninhibited, disbelieving women, the daughters of the Jews.

So where are those of whom Allaah says of them: *"❨ Shall We then treat the (submitting) Muslims like the criminals, polytheists and disbelievers? What is the matter with you? How judge you? ❩*-(Surat al-Qalam, Verses 35-36).

And He, the Most High, says, *❨ Shall We treat those who believe and do righteous good deeds, in the same way as those who associate partners in worship with Allaah and commit crimes) on earth? Or shall We treat the pious as the wicked? ❩*-(Surat Saad, Ayat 28)

And where are they, from the saying of the Messenger, may Allaah's praise and salutations be upon him, *{"They will follow the examples of those who were before them, hand span by hand span, arm span by arm span, until even if they entered the hole of a lizard they would follow them." We said, "Oh Messenger of Allaah, the Jews and the Christians?" He said, "Who else?"}* (Related by al-Bukhaaree (3456) and Muslim (2669), and the wording is Muslim's, from the hadeeth of Abi Sa'eed)

Why do they not use their intellects so that they see the consequences of this dangerous approach? They do not make use of their intelligence, nor are they satisfied with the Book of Allaah and the Sunnah of the Messenger of Allaah, may Allaah's praise and salutations be upon him. They do not emulate the Mothers of the believers, nor do they save themselves from the disbelievers' corrupting them. They are victims of the age. Oh Allaah preserve us, preserve us; for certainly the center of the earth is the lesser in evil from the trials on its surface. Oh Allaah, do not give us cause for remorse, and do not cause us to deviate after You have guided us.

The Call to the Hijaab is Stronger than the Nations and the Political Parties

Two campaigns against the *hijaab* have already been mentioned:

The First: that of the weapons of the tongue and the pens
And the Second: that of the weapons of oppression and force

When the first campaign, with its various categories and classes, was not effective in causing the abandonment of the *hijaab* through looking at the representatives of the western culture, they then instituted the second campaign to defeat the Muslims and cause them to abandon the *hijaab*. There occurred from that those results which occurred, and those who rebelled against Islaam thought that they had accomplished that which they desired from eradicating the *hijaab* forever. But they were taken aback when the love of the legislated *hijaab* increased in many of the Muslim women, and their desire to wear it became intensified, in spite of every malicious person. They were also surprised by the role the Muslim women took in calling to the *hijaab* in their midst. Covered women appeared in areas such as the schools, the universities, and the workplace, They, these women, adhered to the legislated *hijaab* in its entirety. The callers to abandon the *hijaab* were struck by the fact that it led to the women safeguarding Islaam more than before.

In the past some Muslim women wore *hijaab*, however it has come to the point today where she wears the *hijaab* and chooses to adhere to her religion- how many harmful things bring about some benefit! The author of

"'Awdat al-Hijaab" says in his book, (1/289): *"On the anniversary of 100 years of French occupation of Algeria, the French ruler in Algeria said, 'It is obligatory that we eradicate the Arabic Qur'aan from their existence... and wipe out the Arabic language from their tongues, until we become victorious over them.'" A few years after that, France, by way of the defeat of the Qur'aan in the Algerian youth, began an experimental trial, and the selection of ten young Algerian women was completed. The French government enrolled them in French schools, and taught them the French culture, and the French language, until they became completely French. Eleven years after this attempt began, they arranged a party for them as they graduated from the program. Government ministers and intellectuals were invited to it, as well as journalists. When the party began, they were astonished when all of the young Algerian women entered wearing Algerian Islamic clothing. This excited great turmoil in the French newspapers, and they asked: So what has France done in Algeria in the space of 128 years?!?! The minister of the French colony, LaCoste, answered, "And what can I do, if the Qur'aan is stronger than France...?!?!!!"*

The author of *"'Awdat al-Hijaab"* also said, (1/293), *"This, "The Communist People's Journal", is keeping track of the phenomenon in growing anxiety and anger. It has devoted an entire research specifically to this subject, in which is quoted a discussion from Doctor Zaynab Ridwaan. She said, "The hijaab spread amongst the intellectual class before the common people, and this is the opposite of what is traditionally said concerning it. This same intellectual class is that which rejected the hijaab during the time of Hudaa Sha'raawee, and ripped it off and stepped on it. It is the same class which now returned and called to it, and turned back to the truth, with the addition of the fact that the large majority of the women wearing hijaab were from the middle class. This is the class that leads in any society; it is true that the hijaab spread, also,*

> amongst the aristocratic class, but to a proportionately
> lesser degree."

The author also said (1/294): Munaa Ramadaan wrote in October, "*The hijaab has returned once again, as is apparent on the faces of the young and older women in Egypt. This is not another fad in the world of fashion, as one might think at first; rather, it is a form of modesty, and a renewal of Islamic tradition which requires from the women that they bring their jilbaabs close around themselves. Modesty here comes from inside the woman, and on its foundation this garment was founded."*

The return of the Muslim women to wearing the *hijaab* continues in the land of the Muslims, and in other than the land of the Muslims. And what has occurred is that France has taken the lead in establishing laws prohibiting the Muslim women who wear the *hijaab* from attending lessons in the university and other than it, in order to prevent the spreading of the *hijaab*, and the return to it.

From that which proves that the preservation and defense of the *hijaab* has become an issue for the Muslims that cannot be argued with, and which cannot be forced to return to degradation: That which resulted in the general Muslims' condemnation of that which the leader of France, Jacques Cherac, did by prohibiting the Muslim women from wearing the *hijaab* in government places.

And it is as if I stand along with you, oh reader, can you not see how the campaigns against the *hijaab* actually resulted in the call to properly understanding the matter of the *hijaab* and the dedication to preserving it with conviction, not merely as a shallow adoption or a passing illusion? And all praise is for The Most Wise, Most Knowledgeable.

The Third Campaign:

The Campaign to Alter the Islamic Hijaab

*W*hen the secularists, those callers to corrupt the Muslim woman, as well as those others who are proceeding upon their same methodology in battling against the *hijaab* of the Muslim woman, and her clothing- when they have failed in the first two campaigns previously mentioned and their efforts have been wasted, and their faces disgraced- they then resort to a process of changing the *hijaab* itself, little by little, hoping by this to reach a half-*hijaab*, and a *hijaab* which is in conformity with the demands of the degenerates and the low-lifes in the streets. They call for evolution of the clothing for the Muslim woman, under the context of "fashion". Such that the nature of the clothing becomes more ornamental, like the decorated *abayas*, or narrow over garments, and the smaller coverings on the face.

The author of the book, *"Lakay la Yatanaathir al-'Aqd",* says on page 23, that the *"al-Watn"* newspaper recently published a discussion titled, *"An Abaya for the University, the School, the Doctor, the Evening Party, and for Comforting the Bereaved"*, meaning: That the one *abaya* would come to transform into four or more *abayas*. The writer of the book previously ascribed this evolution of the *abaya* to the Muslim woman. However it is actually from the way of the degraded West.

He also quoted, on pages 24-25, *"The first step was the colored abayas. I was the first to create it, and I was the first to start wearing it- I, my mother, and my sister...Also from the most important of my creations was the abaya that had two surfaces: one in one color, (the main one) and the other surface in graduated colors. All of my abayas were made in this form, so that the woman felt that she owned two abayas in one."* Then she adds to the list of her achievements, *"I was the first to include the color of light pink in the abaya, and there is also the "picture" abaya, which has on the inside a professional painting showing a natural scene!"* She uses bright colors on the conventional abayas. She said, *"It is part of my nature that I love going along with the newest thing in fashion. When the Audi B.M. 740 car was introduced, I even utilized the color of that model for an abaya, naming it the "B.M."*"

She also said, on page 25 from the preceding work, *"I believe that there should be an abaya for every occasion. One for the school, another for the university, and one for going to the doctor, and another for the evening party and for wedding parties. I do not see that one abaya is sufficient for all occasions. As for comforting the bereaved, there should be a specific abaya, suitable for the occasion. It is black without any decoration, or color, and it is shut; however, it is fashionable by way of its cut and style."* Then she continued, *"As for an abaya for the wedding party, then it has a cheerful color, and more decorations than any other abaya, and may be the same color as the bride chose for the ballroom and the accoutrements. Likewise, there should be an abaya specifically for the masjid for the month of Ramadhaan. It has close fitting sleeves, and is of a loose style."*

The author of the book also said, on page 21, *"I have read an interview with one of those who participated in designing this new abaya. She is Raphaela Cardinali, an Italian garment designer, when she came to set up a fashion show. She says that her first visit took place in the year 1997; then she made a habit of attending. She expressed her happiness when the fashion show which she established in Riyaadh met with great success. She planned to come here again and again. And under the title it said, "The Appearance of the New Saudi Abaya Competes with International Fashion"*

I say: The following points become clear to the noble readers from this statement:

The creation of different types of *abayas* opens the door to competing in styles of *abaya* and selling it, all based upon that which beautifies them.

Varying the *abayas* with captivating colors, in order to change the *abaya* into attractive and tempting clothing.

The *abayas* are sometimes made short, and sometimes, narrow, and sometimes this, and sometimes that. This is so that the Muslim woman remains smitten by this, at one time, and by that, another time, which causes the Muslim woman to become more and more engaged and to be preoccupied with that which does not accomplish anything for her except to intensify the battle against the legislated *hijaab* and concealing clothing.

The *abayas* have come that are open down the whole length, and in this is a clear evil.

Abayas are made, crowded with rhinestones, embroidery, and various colors. So they become attractive. tempting clothing.

From the Results of this Campaign to Abolish the Hijaab

In actual fact, this call to embellish and change the *hijaab* is in reality a call to abolish the *jilbaab*, which is that which covers the face and body of the woman, with the knowledge that this *jilbaab* is that which Allaah has made obligatory with His saying:

❧ *O Prophet! Tell your wives and your daughters and the women of the believers to draw their cloaks (veils) all over their bodies (i.e. screen themselves completely except the eyes or one eye to see the way). That will be better, that they should be known (as free respectable women) so as not to be harassed. And Allaah is Ever Oft-Forgiving, Most Merciful.* ❧ –(Surah al-Ahzaab, Ayat 59)

When this *fitnah* came, and that is the efforts to change the legislated *hijaab* itself, it caused she who was fascinated by it to in turn become someone who is now alluring and tempting to the people by her wearing it when she goes out. It preoccupied her and she began to choose the most beautiful clothing in order to be seen by the people.

This focus on glamour also resulted in her wearing clothing which she never used to wear around men, and this is the short clothing that stops at the shin, and the sleeves that go only to the upper arm, and the head is uncovered, as well as the throat, and a part of the chest.

From the Calamities Occuring in the Dress of the Muslim Woman

What has become widespread from the wearing of the short overgarment which ends at the middle of the shin, and wearing thin socks through which the ankles and shins can be seen, and then wearing of high heels.

On the whole, this fascination with the clothing is the result of blindly following the disbelieving women by watching the satellite channels. Because of people obtaining these evil devices, the Muslim woman becomes exposed to immorality and nudity. So beware of accepting that which is shown, and that which the Muslim woman is now called to. Rather, it is essential to submit to the Islamic law laid down by Allaah for that which is considered good from the women's dress and beautification, for that which the Islamic law accepts, is accepted, and that which is not accepted by it, is rejected.

As for the woman wearing the *burqa'* (the type of veil worn by many women in Sana'a, in which the eyes show), then from one aspect, it cannot stand in the place of the *jilbaab*, and from another aspect it is a *fitnah*, and how can this not be, if it is combined with a type of beautification!?! For example, the woman using *kohl* to darken her eyes, and then her eyes are visible through the opening of the veil; thus the veil becomes a great *fitnah* because of that which is not covered.

The Legislated Rules for the Muslim Women's Hijaab and her Clothing

The Muslim woman must know that the issue of *hijaab* and clothing she wears is not one simply dependent upon one's inclination and desires, or the frivolous ideas of those who are of weak morals, or the deception of the scheming deceivers. Indeed, this thinking is from that which destroys the laws laid down by Allaah, which includes guidelines that it is not permissible to neglect or corrupt.

From these proof is the saying of Allaah, the Most High, ❖*... and to draw their veils all over Juyubihinna (i.e. their bodies, faces, necks and bosoms, etc.)*❖–(Surat an-Noor, Ayat 31)

It is narrated in *"Saheeh al-Bukhaaree"*, Number 4758, on 'Aishah, may Allaah be pleased with her, that she said, *{May Allaah bestow His mercy upon the women of the Muhaajiraat (the women who emigrated from Mecca to Medina), who were the first to rip their muroot (woolen dress-like garments) and cover themselves with them when the Ayat "and to draw their veils all over juyubihinna" was revealed.}*

Al-Haafidh ibn Haajir said in *"Fath al-Baaree"* (8/628) concerning the word "فاختمرن» (and cover themselves), "That is to say, they covered their faces, and that is specifically: to put the *khimaar* (scarf) over her head, and to toss it from the right side to the left shoulder, and it is to be veiled. Al-Faraa' said, 'In the times of ignorance before Islaam, the woman let her *khimaar* hang down from her back, and uncovered her front. Thus she is commanded to cover herself.'"

And it is authenticated from her ('Aishah, may Allaah be pleased with her), that she explained the saying of The Most High, ❖ *...and not to show off their* *adornment except only that which is apparent* –(Surah an-Noor, Ayat 31). She said, *{(This is referring to) the clothes, not the face or hands.}*

And the Most High said, *O Prophet! Tell your wives and your daughters and the women of the believers to draw their cloaks (veils) all over their bodies (i.e. screen themselves completely except the eyes or one eye to see the way). That will be better, that they should be known (as free respectable women) so as not to be harassed. And Allaah is Ever Oft-Forgiving, Most Merciful.*-(Surat al-Ahzaab, Ayat 59).

The female companions, the mothers of the believers, and whose who followed them understood that to mean, to lower the *khimaar* over the face. It is related on Sa'eed ibn Mansoor, as found in *"Fath al-Bari"* (3/517) with an authentic chain of narration, on 'Aishah, that she said, *{The woman lowered her jilbaab from over her head and over her face. This was prevalent amongst all of the women.}*

At the time of the Prophet, may Allaah's praise and salutations be upon him and his family, and his companions, the women's *jilbaabs* were black. It is narrated on Umm Salamah, may Allaah be pleased with her, that she said, *{ When the verse " draw their cloaks (veils) all over their bodies" was revealed, the women of the Ansaar went out and it was as if on their heads were crows, from what they were wearing.}* This is narrated in Abu Daawood, Number 4101, and its chain of narration is authentic.

It is proper for the woman's clothing to cover all of her body. It is narrated on 'Abdullah ibn 'Umar, may Allaah be pleased with him, that he said,*{ The Messenger of Allaah, may Allaah's praise and salutations be upon him, said, "Allaah will not look (on the Day of Resurrection) at him who trails his garment out of arrogance." Umm Salamah, (the wife of* *the Prophet, may Allaah's praise and salutations be upon him), may Allaah be pleased with her, said, "Oh Messenger of Allaah, what should the woman do with the train of her garment?" He said, "Lower it a hand span." She said, "What if her feet are uncovered?" He said, "Then lower it an arm span, and do not increase upon that."}* (An-Nasaa'i narrated it (number 5336), and the hadeeth Umm Salamah is found in an-Nasaa'i as well (number 5337))

The hadeeth is clear, that it is obligatory upon the woman to cover her feet in the situation where she is out amongst those who are not considered *mahram* for her. The scholars have concluded from it that it is obligatory for the face to be covered with greater reason, because the sight of the face is a greater *fitnah* (trial) than the sight of the feet.

It is not permissible for the Muslim woman to wear garments made of thin, flimsy fabric through which her skin can be seen when leaving her house, It is related from Abu Hurairah, may Allaah be pleased with him, that he said,*{ The Messenger of Allaah, may Allaah's praise and salutations be upon him, said, "There are two groups amongst the people of the Hellfire: A people who have with them whips, like the tails of the ox, who strike the people with them. (The second one) is the women who would be naked in spite of their being dressed, who are seduced (to wrong paths) and seduce others with their hair high like humps. These women would not get into Paradise and they would not smell its scent, although its fragrance can be perceived from such and such distance."}* (Collected in Muslim, Number 2128)

The scholars have mentioned conditions for the *hijaab* along with what has been mentioned.

From them:

That it does not resemble the clothing of the disbelievers, and does not resemble the clothing of the men. It cannot be a dress of fame, nor can it be adorned. It cannot have crosses on it, or pictures of those living things that have souls, and cannot be perfumed. They present the proofs for these stated conditions.

So beware, beware of the Muslim woman neglecting acting upon and adhering to these tremendous rules of conduct. The Muslim woman must adhere to wearing gloves when she goes out amongst men who are not *mahram* for her. This is because the Prophet, may Allaah's praise and salutations be upon him, said concerning the dress of the female pilgrim going to *Hajj* who has entered the state of *ihram*, or consecration, *{Do not wear a veil, and do not wear gloves }* This is transmitted by al-Bukhaaree, from Ibn 'Umar. This is proof that those other than the ones in *ihraam* do indeed wear them.

In summary it is said: The woman must wear the enveloping *hijaab*, which covers the whole of her body, including her face and her hands.

To learn more about this, read my work, "*al-Akhtaa' al-Muta'adidah fee Hajj al-Mara'at al-Mutabarajah*", which has been published, and all praise and goodness belongs to Allaah.

The Pride of the Western Muslim Woman in Hijaab

Allaah says in His Noble Book, ❧ *And if you turn away (from Islaam and the obedience of Allaah), He will exchange you for some other people, and they will not be your likes.* ❧-(Surat Muhammad, Ayat 38)

And He says, ❧ *O you who believe! Whoever from among you turns back from his religion (Islaam), Allaah will bring a people whom He will love and they will love Him; humble towards the believers, stern towards the disbelievers, fighting in the Way of Allaah, and never afraid of the blame of the blamers. That is the Grace of Allaah which He bestows on whom He wills. And Allaah is All-Sufficient for His creatures' needs, All-Knower.* ❧-(Surat al-Maa'idah, Ayat 54).

Already in the West the women are entering into Islaam day and night, and proceeding to hold fast to it, and implementing its rulings, and conforming to its prescribed standards of behavior. From that is their compliance with the *hijaab* and their understanding of its exaltedness, and happiness comes to them by reason of it. The Muslim woman must listen to what her Western sister has to say from that which is good:

The author of the book, *"Lakay la Yatanaathir al-'Aqd"*, pages 77-79, says, "*These are a number of Western women who have tasted the flavor of faith, and the pleasure of uprightness on this way of life, they say one after another,*

The hijaab increases me in true beauty.

> *The hijaab is a public statement of commitment to the religion.*

The hijaab is a symbol of freedom.

The hijaab supplies me with added protection.

When I embraced Islaam, I made up my mind to wear the complete hijaab, from my head to my feet.

The hijaab is a part of me, of my very nature, as I began to wear it shortly before I embraced Islaam because it made me feel that I am respecting myself when I wear it."

He (the author) also said, on page 79, that which a Greek woman, Therese, said to him. "*I don't wish to speak, as my happiness with Islaam cannot be described ever. If you were to write books, and volumes, it would not be sufficient to describe my emotions and my happiness. I am Muslim, Muslim, Muslim! Say to all the people: I am Muslim, and I am happy with my Islaam. Say to them, by every means of informing by way of the media: Therese al-Yoonaaniyah became Khadijah in her religion, her clothing, her actions, and her way of thinking.*"

Here is Zeefreed Hawanakah, the author of the book, "*The Arabian Sun Shines on the West*". She was asked in one of the meetings, what is her advice to the Arab woman who wishes to be rid of the *hijaab*?

She replied, "*She should not take the European, American, or Russian woman as an example, and imitate her, or be guided by an ideological plot, no matter what its source. This is because in that is a new fixation on the foreign way of thought, which results in her losing her individual values. That which is necessary upon her is to adhere to the guidance of the fundamental Islaam, and to conduct herself in the manner of those who have preceded her from the righteous predecessors, those who lead the life which has as a base the laws of nature which have been created for her."* Taken from the book, *"Lakay la Yatanaathir al'-Aqd"*, page 82.

Here an Arabian Muslim woman takes valuable advice from her foreign Muslim sister. The story is mentioned by the author of the book, *"Lakay la Yatanaathir al'-Aqd"*, page 90. It is:

The Arab Muslimah says, *"Once I travelled to a foreign country, and I was not satisfied with merely beautifying and adorning my hijaab; rather, I took it off, and tossed it into the seat of the plane in which I was travelling. In that country my eyes were drawn to a woman who was wearing hijaab. You could not see anything of her at all. Her abaaya (overgarment) was long and very wide. Her scarf was long, and hung down low. I approached her, as I heard her speaking in a foreign language. I was completely astonished... I asked myself, "She appears to be an Arab woman, yet she has acquired the language of the people, and she speaks it fluently and with great capability!?!?" My curiosity drove me forward, as I tossed a question to her: "Are you an Arab?" "No. I am a Canadian Muslimah. I embraced Islaam a year and a half ago, and ever since then I have been as you see me. I wear my hijaab, and go on my way, and my self-respect and my sense of honor with my new religion go with me!" I put my hand on my head, to find my scarf... I did not find it. I remembered that I had thrown it onto the seat of the airplane. I repeated warm words between me and my soul (to myself)..."Oh Allaah... Oh Lord...is this foreign woman, who has not known You or believed in You except for only a year and a half, and I...I...my grandfather is Muslim, my father is Muslim, and my mother, and by brother...indeed, my people are all Muslim.. I grew up upon obedience to You, and was brought up in a house in where the people believed in You. So how is it that I so easily abandoned my hijaab, and she adheres to You with it!?!?"*

Another Arab woman received a great lesson from her foreign sister. The Arab woman said, *"I went with my husband to France. I had with me at that time a long garment, and a head covering. I entered a large masjid in Paris and performed the prayer. At the door of the masjid I became uneasy about leaving, and removed my head covering and long garment. I was worried about putting them in the bag, and here I had a surprise. I was approached by a young French woman with blue eyes. I shall never forget her as long as I live. She was wearing the hijaab... She held my hand with kindness, and patted me on the shoulder, and said in a soft voice, "Why do you take off the hijaab? Don't you know that it is Allaah's command...?!! I was listening to her absently, and she implored me to enter the masjid with her for a few minutes. I tried to break away from her, but her very good manners and her kind speech compelled me to enter. She asked me, "Do you bear witness that there is no God worthy of being worshipped except Allaah? Do you understand its meaning? Truly, they are not words just said with the tongue; rather, they are from belief and action..." This young woman taught me a hard lesson in life; my heart trembled and my emotions submitted to her words. She then shook hands with me, and said, "My sister, stand up for this religion." I left the masjid, immersed in thought, unaware of my surroundings..."* Excerpted from *"Lakay la Yatanaathir al-'Aqd"*, pages 91-92.

Here is the British journalist Yvonne Ridley, who was taken into custody by the Taalibaan movement during her attempt to enter Afghaanistaan in October of 2001. She was afterwards released and later announced her (embracing) Islaam. She criticized the charge of the Egyptian Minister of culture on the *hijaab* in a lecture given as part of the activities of "*The Tenth Conference of the International Association of Muslim Youth*", which was organized in Cairo. She said, "*Truly, those Arabs who wish to be Westerners in their behavior, more so than the foreigners themselves; they incite scorn in others.*" And from the strange things she mentioned was, "The last time I visited here in Cairo, I was finally labeled as an extremist. The accusation came to me from a Sheikh from al-Azhar University (Doctor Muhammad Sayyid Tantaawee), because, when he extended his hand to greet me, I refused to shake it, in observance of the Islamic law. So he said to me, 'You are an extremist.'" This is quoted from "Majalat al-Bayaan", Number 232, from Dhu al-Hijjah, 1427 hijree.

Indeed, even the Western disbelieving women admire the hijaab, as demonstrated by this English writer who went to Egypt in the beginning of the twentieth century and resided there for months, mingling with the Muslim women who wore hijaab. She returned deeply affected by the beautiful condition of the Muslim woman. She wrote an article entitled, "A Question Conveyed from the East, to the Western Woman". She wrote, "If this freedom that we have finally attained, and this competition in enjoying that which is forbidden, and ridding the genders of the fascinating, stimulating, barriers which are by nature established between the two...if the end result of all this is that the man still has power over the woman, and everything that stirs the strings of marital love is removed from the heart, then what have we gained? By God, this condition has made it necessary for us to change our course; in fact, we should voluntarily remain behind the Eastern covering in order to relearn the art of love." From "Lakay la Yatanaathr al-'Aqd", page 115.

The American writer Hillson said, in the previously mentioned work, page 87, after she spent several weeks in one of the Arab capitals and returned to her country, "The Arab society is complete and perfect. It is appropriate for this society to adhere to its traditions, as it holds the young men and women within the bounds of that which is reasonable. For you have an inherent moral character which necessitates that the woman has limits, and necessitates respect towards the parents, and more than that, it necessitates that *there be none of the Western licentiousness which is today destroying the European and American society and family. So forbid intermixing, and restrict the young women's freedom; rather, return to the time of the hijaab, as this is better for you all than licentiousness and uninhibitedness, and the shamelessness of Europe and America."*

Oh Muslim woman: I have been overlong in this account, and these mentioned reports make an impact on the men who read them- and so how can they not fill the heart of the Muslim woman who plays around with her religion with sorrow, regret, sadness, and blame for herself? Considering that there results from her actions, in the view of Islaam, that which blackens her face, and lowers her status, even though she is a daughter of Islaam; drinking from it, and is nourished by it morning and evening.

So it is necessary, Oh Muslim women, to take another look, before it is too late, before leaving this life in which the material gain and profit has been made easy, to a Hereafter of true loss, and before the standing in front of the All-Knower of the secrets and of that which is in the hearts, the Commander of guidance and piety, and the Warner against following the desires. The Warner against one in whom obedience to him is every affliction- and that is only the accursed *Shaytaan*, who calls to every sort of evil, which leads to the Blazing Fire. Yet turning to Allaah in repentance is the pathway which leads one from the darkness into the light, and from wickedness to delight, may Allaah grant success to all in all that is good.

It is upon the rulers of Muslim nations to forbid the unlawful uncovering and the unveiling of the face. It is mandatory to know that it is obligatory upon those who are responsible, from the leaders, and

the ministers, and the government, to forbid the
unlawful uncovering and the unveiling of the face,
as well as the mixing between the women and the men.

Sheikh al-Islaam Ibn Taymiyyah, may Allaah have mercy
upon him, said, as found in *"Majmoo' al-Fataawa"*, 24/382,
"*The women uncovering their faces where the people who are
not mahram to them can see them is not permissible, and it is
upon those who are responsible (such as the rulers) That they
command the good, and forbid this and other evils. And the
one who does not respond should be punished with that which
would restrain him.*"

Imaam Ibn-Qayyim, may Allaah have mercy upon him,
said, in *"at-Turuq al-Hakamiyyah"*, page 280, "*From that is
that it is obligatory on the one who is responsible to forbid the
intermixing of the men and the women, in the markets, and
those places where the men gather.*"

Maalik, may Allaah have mercy upon him, said, "*As I see it,
it is for the Imaam, meaning the general leader of the Muslims,
to go out to the craftspeople amongst whom the women sit, and
he should not allow the young woman to sit with them, as the
Imaam is responsible for that, and the fitnah that comes with it
is great. The Messenger, may Allaah's prayers and good mention
be upon him, said, {There will not be a trial left behind after me more
harmful for the men, than the women.} ("Saheeh al-Bukhaaree")*"

And in another hadeeth, that he, may Allaah's prayers and
good mention be upon him, said to the women, { *For you is
the side of the pathway to walk upon.*} (Abu Daawud, and Ibn
Hibban by meaning, see Number 38 of "Fifty Hadeeth…"
for full information)"

It is obligatory upon him to prevent the women from going out uncovered and beautified, and to forbid for them the clothing by which she is dressed, yet naked, such as that which is flowing and flimsy. He must forbid them from needlessly speaking to the men in the street, and forbid the men from that practice as well.

If the one who is responsible, the governmental authorities, decide to ruin the clothing of she who goes out adorned and beautified with ink and the like, then some of the scholars of jurisprudence permit that, and it stands as correct. And this is from at least financial punishment for her actions.

It is upon him to confine the woman, if she leaves her house excessively, specifically if she goes out impermissibly beautified. Allowing the woman to do that is supporting her in sin and wrongdoing. Allaah will question the one responsible concerning that.

The commander of the faithful, 'Umar ibn al-Khataab, may Allaah be pleased with him, forbade the women from walking in the path of the men and mixing with them in the street. So it is upon the one who is responsible to follow his example in that.

Many of the Muslim governments neglect this issue, and this is significant negligence on their part. This is when they have themselves accepted the call to uncovering, and unveiling the face, and so they allow the mixing of the women and the men. This behavior from them is a prominent reason for the spreading of corruption, which contributes to the ruin of the nation and of the punishment of Allaah coming down, and the suffering on the society which is enthralled and enamored with wrongdoing.

The state of the Muslim rulers now, by reason of this negligence, does not bring glad tidings; for how many times they have been defeated by others, and how many have dominance over them from the Jews and Christians And there is no change nor strength except through Allaah. They must return to their Lord, and hold fast to their religion, and restore that which they have corrupted, and bring about that which they have left from the good.

All glory and praise is to Allaah, there is no god worthy of worship except for him, and I ask You for forgiveness and I repent to You.

The Nakhlah Educational Series: Mission and Methodology (Pocket Edition)

Mission

The Purpose of the 'Nakhlah Educational Series' is to contribute to the present knowledge based efforts which enable Muslim individuals, families, and communities to understand and learn Islaam and then to develop within and truly live Islaam. Our commitment and goal is to contribute beneficial publications and works that:

Firstly, reflect the priority, message and methodology of all the prophets and messengers sent to humanity, meaning that single revealed message which embodies the very purpose of life, and of human creation. As Allaah the Most High has said,

❀ *We sent a Messenger to every nation ordering them that they should worship Allaah alone, obey Him and make their worship purely for Him, and that they should avoid everything worshipped besides Allaah. So from them there were those whom Allaah guided to His religion, and there were those who were unbelievers for whom misguidance was ordained. So travel through the land and see the destruction that befell those who denied the Messengers and disbelieved.* ❀ —(Surah an-Nahl: 36)

Two Essential Foundations

Secondly, building upon the above foundation, our commitment is to contributing publications and works which reflect the inherited message and methodology of the acknowledged scholars of the many various branches of Sharee'ah knowledge who stood upon the straight path of preserved guidance in every century and time since the time of our Messenger, may Allaah's praise and salutations be upon him. These people of knowledge, who are the inheritors of the Final Messenger, have always adhered closely to the two revealed sources of guidance: the Book of Allaah and the Sunnah of the Messenger of Allaah- may Allaah's praise and salutations be upon him, upon the united consensus, standing with the body of guided Muslims in every century - preserving and transmitting the true religion generation after generation. Indeed the Messenger of Allaah, may Allaah's praise and salutations be upon him, informed us that, *{ A group of people amongst my Ummah will remain obedient to Allaah's orders. They will not be harmed by those who leave them nor by those who oppose them, until Allaah's command for the Last Day comes upon them while they remain on the right path. }* (Authentically narrated in Saheeh al-Bukhaaree).

The guiding scholar Sheikh Zayd al-Madkhalee, may Allaah protect him, stated in his writing, 'The Well Established Principles of the Way of the First Generations of Muslims: It's Enduring & Excellent Distinct Characteristics' that,

"From among these principles and characteristics is that the methodology of tasfeeyah -or clarification, and tarbeeyah -or education and cultivation- is clearly affirmed and established as a true way coming from the first three generations of Islaam, and is something well known to the people of true merit from among them, as is concluded by considering all the related evidence. What is intended by tasfeeyah, when referring to it generally, is clarifying that which is the truth from that which is falsehood, what is goodness from that which is harmful and corrupt, and when referring to its specific meanings it is distinguishing the noble Sunnah of the Prophet and the people of the Sunnah from those innovated matters brought into the religion and the people who are supporters of such innovations.

As for what is intended by tarbeeyah, it is calling all of the creation to take on the manners and embrace the excellent character invited to by that guidance revealed to them by their

Lord through His worshiper and Messenger Muhammad, may Allaah's praise and salutations be upon him; so that they might have good character, manners, and behavior. As without this they cannot have a good life, nor can they put right their present condition or their final destination. And we seek refuge in Allaah from the evil of not being able to achieve that rectification."

Thus the methodology of the people of standing upon the Prophet's Sunnah, and proceeding upon the 'way of the believers' in every century is reflected in a focus and concern with these two essential matters: tasfeeyah or clarification of what is original, revealed message from the Lord of all the worlds, and tarbeeyah or education and raising of ourselves, our families, and our communities, and our lands upon what has been distinguished to be that true message and path.

Methodology:

The Roles of the Scholars & General Muslims In Raising the New Generation

The priority and focus of the 'Nakhlah Educational Series' is reflected within in the following statements of Sheikh al-Albaanee, may Allaah have mercy upon him:

"As for the other obligation, then I intend by this the education of the young generation upon Islaam purified from all of those impurities we have mentioned, giving them a correct Islamic education from their very earliest years, without any influence of a foreign, disbelieving education."

(Silsilat al-Hadeeth ad-Da'eefah, Introduction page 2.)

"...And since the Messenger of Allaah, may Allaah's praise and salutations be upon him, has indicated that the only cure to remove this state of humiliation that we find ourselves entrenched within, is truly returning back to the religion. Then it is clearly

obligatory upon us - through the people of knowledge- to correctly and properly understand the religion in a way that conforms to the sources of the Book of Allaah and the Sunnah, and that we educate and raise a new virtuous, righteous generation upon this."

(Clarification and Cultivation and the Need of the Muslims for Them)

It is essential in discussing our perspective upon this obligation of raising the new generation of Muslims, that we highlight and bring attention to a required pillar of these efforts as indicated by Sheikh al-Albaanee, may Allaah have mercy upon him, and others- in the golden words, *"through the people of knowledge"*. Since something we commonly experience today is that many people have various incorrect understandings of the role that the scholars should have in the life of a Muslim, failing to understand the way in which they fulfill their position as the inheritors of the Messenger of Allaah, may Allaah's praise and salutations be upon him, and stand as those who preserve and enable us to practice the guidance of Islaam.   Similarly the guiding scholar Sheikh 'Abdul-'Azeez Ibn Baaz, may Allaah have mercy upon him, also emphasized this same overall responsibility:

*"...It is also upon a Muslim that he struggles diligently in that which will place his worldly affairs in a good state, just as he must also strive in the correcting of his religious affairs and the affairs of his own family. As the people of his household have a significant right over him that he strive diligently in rectifying their affair and guiding them towards goodness, due to the statement of Allaah, the Most Exalted, ◌ **Oh you who believe! Save yourselves and your families Hellfire whose fuel is men and stones** ◌ -(Surah at-Tahreem: 6)*

So it is upon you to strive to correct the affairs of the members of your family. This includes your wife, your children- both male and female- and such as your own brothers. This concerns all of the people in your family, meaning you should strive to teach them the religion, guiding and directing them, and warning them from those matters Allaah has prohibited for us. Because you are the one who is responsible for them as shown in the statement of the Prophet, may Allaah's praise and salutations be upon him, *{ Every one of you is a guardian, and responsible for what is in his custody. The ruler is a guardian of his subjects and responsible for them; a husband is a guardian of his family and is responsible for it; a lady is a guardian of her husband's house and is responsible for it, and a servant is a guardian of his master's property and is responsible for it....}* Then the Messenger of Allaah, may Allaah's praise and salutations be upon him, continued to say, *{...so all of you are guardians and are responsible for those under your authority.}* (Authentically narrated in Saheeh al-Bukhaaree & Muslim)

It is upon us to strive diligently in correcting the affairs of the members of our families, from the aspect of purifying their sincerity of intention for Allaah's sake alone in all of their deeds, and ensuring that they truthfully believe in and follow the Messenger of Allaah, may Allaah's praise and salutations be upon him, their fulfilling the prayer and the other obligations which Allaah the Most Exalted has commanded for us, as well as from the direction of distancing them from everything which Allaah has prohibited.

It is upon every single man and women to give advice to their families about the fulfillment of what is obligatory upon them. Certainly, it is upon the woman as well as upon the man to perform this. In this way our homes become corrected and rectified in regard to the most important and essential matters. Allaah said to His Prophet, may Allaah's praise and salutations be upon him, ﴾ *And enjoin the ritual prayers on your family...* ﴿ (Surah Taha: 132) Similarly, Allaah the Most Exalted said to

His prophet Ismaa'aeel, ◈ ***And mention in the Book, Ismaa'aeel. Verily, he was true to what he promised, and he was a Messenger, and a Prophet. And he used to enjoin on his family and his people the ritual prayers and the obligatory charity, and his Lord was pleased with him.*** ◈ *-(Surah Maryam: 54-55)*

As such, it is only proper that we model ourselves after the prophets and the best of people, and be concerned with the state of the members of our households. Do not be neglectful of them, oh worshipper of Allaah! Regardless of whether it is concerning your wife, your mother, father, grandfather, grandmother, your brothers, or your children; it is upon you to strive diligently in correcting their state and condition..."

(Collection of Various Rulings and Statements- Sheikh 'Abdul-'Azeez Ibn 'Abdullah Ibn Baaz, Vol. 6, page 47)

Content & Structure:

We hope to contribute works which enable every striving Muslim who acknowledges the proper position of the scholars, to fulfill the recognized duty and obligation which lays upon each one of us to bring the light of Islaam into our own lives as individuals as well as into our homes and among our families. Towards this goal we are committed to developing educational publications and comprehensive educational curriculums -through cooperation with and based upon the works of the scholars of Islaam and the students of knowledge. Works which, with the assistance of Allaah, the Most High, we can utilize to educate and instruct ourselves, our families and our communities upon Islaam in both principle and practice. The publications and works of the Nakhlah Educational Series are divided into the following categories:

Basic: Ages 4- 6

Elementary: Ages 6-11

Secondary: Ages 11-14

High School: Ages 14- Young Adult

General: Young Adult –Adult

Supplementary: All Ages

Publications and works within these stated levels will, with the permission of Allaah, encompass different beneficial areas and subjects, and will be offered in every permissible form of media and medium. As certainly, as the guiding scholar Sheikh Saaleh Fauzaan al-Fauzaan, may Allaah preserve him, has stated,

"Beneficial knowledge is itself divided into two categories. Firstly is that knowledge which is tremendous in its benefit, as it benefits in this world and continues to benefit in the Hereafter. This is religious Sharee'ah knowledge. And secondly, that which is limited and restricted to matters related to the life of this world, such as learning the processes of manufacturing various goods. This is a category of knowledge related specifically to worldly affairs.

…As for the learning of worldly knowledge, such as knowledge of manufacturing, then it is legislated upon us collectively to learn whatever the Muslims have a need for. Yet If they do not have a need for this knowledge, then learning it is a neutral matter upon the condition that it does not compete with or displace any areas of Sharee'ah knowledge…"

("Explanations of the Mistakes of Some Writers"", Pages 10-12)

We ask Allaah, the most High to bless us with success in contributing to the many efforts of our Muslim brothers and sisters committed to raising themselves as individuals and the next generation of our children upon that Islaam which Allaah has perfected and chosen for us, and which He has enabled the guided Muslims to proceed upon in each and every century. We ask him to forgive us, and forgive the Muslim men and the Muslim women, and to guide all the believers to everything He loves and is pleased with. The success is from Allaah, The Most High The Most Exalted, alone and all praise is due to Him.

Abu Sukhailah Khalil Ibn-Abelahyi
Taalib al-Ilm Educational Resources

BOOK PUBLICATION PREVIEW:

Statements of the Guiding Scholars of Our Age Regarding Books & their Advice to the Beginner Seeker of Knowledge

with Selections from the Following Scholars:

Sheikh 'Abdul-'Azeez ibn 'Abdullah ibn Baaz -Sheikh Muhammad ibn Saaleh al-'Utheimein - Sheikh Muhammad Naasiruddeen al-Albaanee - Sheikh Muqbil ibn Haadee al-Waada'ee - Sheikh 'Abdur-Rahman ibn Naaser as-Sa'adee - Sheikh Muhammad 'Amaan al-Jaamee - Sheikh Muhammad al-Ameen as-Shanqeetee - Sheikh Ahmad ibn Yahya an-Najmee & Sheikh Saaleh al-Fauzaan ibn 'Abdullah al-Fauzaan - Sheikh Saaleh ibn 'Abdul-'Azeez Aal-Sheikh - Sheikh Muhammad ibn 'Abdul-Wahhab al-Wasaabee -Permanent Committee to Scholastic Research & Issuing Of Islamic Rulings

With an introduction by: Sheikh Muhammad Ibn 'Abdullah al-Imaam

Collected and Translated by Abu Sukhailah Khalil Ibn-Abelahyi al-Amreekee

[Available: **Now** ¦ pages: 370+ ¦ price: (S) **$25**

(H) **$32** ¦ eBook **$9.99**]

SCAN WITH SMARTPHONE

PRINT

FOR MORE INFORMATION

SCAN WITH SMARTPHONE

EBOOK

FOR MORE INFORMATION

BOOK PUBLICATION PREVIEW:

Fasting from Alif to Yaa:

A Day by Day Guide to Making the Most of Ramadhaan

-Contains additional points of benefit to teach one how to live Islaam as a way of life
-Plus, stories of the Prophets and Messengers including activities for the whole family to enjoy and benefit from for each day of Ramadhaan. Some of the Prophets and Messengers covered include Aadam, Ibraaheem, Lut, Yusuf, Sulaymaan, Shu'ayb, Moosa, Zakariyyah, Muhammad, and more! -Recipes for foods enjoyed by Muslims around the world

By Umm Mujaahid Khadijah Bint Lacina al-Amreekiyyah as-Salafiyyah With Abu Hamzah Hudhaifah Ibn Khalil and Umm Usaamah Sukhailah Bint Khalil

[Available: **1433** -pages: 250+ ¦ price: (S) **$20** (H) **$27** ¦ eBook **$9.99**

SCAN WITH SMARTPHONE

PRINT

FOR MORE INFORMATION

SCAN WITH SMARTPHONE

EBOOK

FOR MORE INFORMATION

BOOK PUBLICATION PREVIEW:

My Home, My Path

A Comprehensive Source Book For Today's Muslim Woman Discussing Her Essential Role & Contribution To The Establishment of Islaam – Taken From The Words Of The People Of Knowledge

Collected and Translated by
Umm Mujaahid Khadijah Bint Lacina
al-Amreekiyyah

[Available: **Now** ¦ pages: **420+** ¦ price: (Soft cover) **$22.50**
(Hard cover) **$29.50** (eBook) **$9.99**]

BOOK PUBLICATION PREVIEW:

Thalaathatu al-Usool: The Three Fundamental Principles

A Step by Step Educational Course on Islaam
Based upon Commentaries of 'Thalaathatu al-Usool'
of Sheikh Muhammad ibn 'Abdul Wahaab
(may Allaah have mercy upon him)

*Collected and Arranged by Umm Mujaahid
Khadijah Bint Lacina al-Amreekiyyah*

Description:

*A complete course for the Believing men and women
who want to learn their religion from the ground
up, building a firm foundation upon which to base
their actions. This is the* **second** *in our* **Foundation
Series** *on Islamic beliefs and making them a reality
in your life, which began with* **"al-Waajibaat: The
Obligatory Matters".**

[Available: **Now Self Study/ Teachers Edition** ¦
price: (Soft cover) **$22.50** (Hard cover) **$29.50**
Directed Study Edition price: (S) **$17.50** -
Exercise Workbook price: (S) **$10** ¦ eBook **$9.99**]

SCAN WITH SMARTPHONE

PRINT

FOR MORE INFORMATION

SCAN WITH SMARTPHONE

EBOOK

FOR MORE INFORMATION

BOOK PUBLICATION PREVIEW:

Whispers of Paradise (1): A Muslim Woman's Life Journal

An Islamic Daily Journal Which Encourages Reflection & Rectification

Collected and Edited by Taalib al-Ilm Educational Resources Development Staff

[Available: **Now** ¦ price: (Hard cover) **$32**]
[Elegantly designed edition is for the year 1434 / 2013]

12 Monthly calendar pages with beneficial quotations from Ibn Qayyim
Daily journal page based upon Islamic calendar (with corresponding C.E. dates)

SCAN WITH SMARTPHONE

FOR MORE INFORMATION

BOOK PUBLICATION PREVIEW:

The Cure, The Explanation, The Clear Affair, & The Brilliantly Distinct Signpost

A Step by Step Educational Course on Islaam Based upon Commentaries of

'Usul as-Sunnah' of Imaam Ahmad
(may Allaah have mercy upon him)

Study of text divided into chapters formatted into multiple short lessons to facilitate learning . Each lesson has: evidence summary, lesson benefits, standard & review exercises 'Usul as-Sunnah' Arabic text & translation divided for easier memorization.

Compiled and Translated by:
Abu Sukhailah Khalil Ibn-Abelahyi

[Available: **TBA** ¦ price: **TBA** (Multi-volume) ¦ soft cover, hard cover, ebook]

SCAN WITH SMARTPHONE

PRINT

FOR MORE INFORMATION

SCAN WITH SMARTPHONE

EBOOK

FOR MORE INFORMATION

Made in the USA
Las Vegas, NV
24 May 2025

22625746R00069